A LETTER TO TRISH

Life as a Jarrell in the Early 20th Century

Patricia Ackerman

A LETTER TO TRISH
Copyright © 2016 by Patricia Ackerman.

Library of Congress Control Number: 2016945304
ISBN: Paperback   978-1-68256-927-6
               PDF   978-1-68256-928-3
               ePub   978-1-68256-929-0
               Kindle   978-1-68256-930-6

This is a documentary of a young girl growing up in rural Georgia in the early 20th Century.

Printed in the United States of America.

LitFire LLC
1-800-511-9787
www.litfirepublishing.com
order@litfirepublishing.com

Contents

Acknowledgements

Special thanks to:

Edmund Bernosky
Many photos of the Jarrell Plantation were taken by Edmund Bernosky.

Ricky and Paulette Montgomery
Some photos of the Jarrell Plantation were taken by Ricky and Paulette Montgomery.

And

Ruth Riggs
Other photos of the Jarrell Plantation were taken by Ruth Riggs.

Beatrice Jarrell Bittaker
Gray High School Graduation 1930
Valedictorian
Jones County, Georgia

Forward by Edmund Bernosky
Son-in law of Bea Bittaker

In 1974, the Jarrell Plantation was donated to the State of Georgia. It is now a State Historic Site.

It was a middle class plantation and can be seen in its original setting. It was owned and operated by the same family for over 140 years. This plantation survived all through the years, through typhoid fever, diphtheria, General Sherman's "March to the Sea," Emancipation, Reconstruction and the cotton boll weevil.

Visitors can see all the structures and dwellings which were handmade by the family. Among such are the sawmill, cotton gin, blacksmith's shop and smoke house. John Fitz Jarrell built a home in 1847 which was typical of a home on a middle class plantation.

John's son, Dick Jarrell, built a home in 1895. This home, with much of its homemade furnishings can also be seen. This small home housed 11 children.

It has been said that the Jarrell Plantation is one of the finest surviving examples of a typical "middle class" southern plantation.

Dick Jarrell's children were the last of the Jarrell family to work the farm. The 11th child of twelve children was Beatrice (Bea) Jarrell born in 1912.

Bea recalls her childhood growing up on this farm. She shares her personal experiences using her vivid memory in order to offer readers a wealth of little known everyday occurrences of a lifestyle that is now defunct for the most part. With her very descriptive vocabulary she brings to life a narrative of this southern middle class plantation living.

The narrative created by her is written in such a way that it provides an enjoyable, informative and fun reading for anyone at any level.

Trish:

When you asked me to write down some of the memoirs of my life, I thought, "That will be relatively easy. Perhaps I shall be able to write ten or twelve pages."

Thank you for making this request. As I began to write, more and more memories surfaced in my mind. As you see now, I have a sizable biography.

There are so many ways of living about which you may be dubious, but my two living siblings will verify its veracity. There are responsibilities and ways of life that I had that would be considered life-enduring. With new inventions and new ways of performing duties, many of these ways are now defunct. I want my children and descendants to know about these things. I want you to know of our hardships and limitations in these everyday happenings. I am not attempting to evoke pity but to see how these limitations were lessons in helping us to overcome obstacles.

About some of the contends of this manuscript, I have consulted with not-related women who were born in this era that the happenings were prevalent.

Truly, I hope that you and my rising generations will enjoy it.

Patricia Ackerman

JARRELL PLANTATION
1920 Jarrell House
Juliette, Georgia

A LETTER TO TRISH

From her mother,
Beatrice Jarrell Bittaker

JARRELL PLANTATION
1920 Jarrell House
Juliette, Georgia

Jarrell Girls   East side of
1920 House

Back, L/R, Bessie, Allyne, Sarah,
Front, L/R, Beatrice and Mildred

THE EARLY LIFE AND TIMES OF BEA JARRELL BITTAKER

HOME

Papa built the home with the wood that he milled himself and with the nails he made.

The brick chimney was hand-made by Papa.

In touring the plantation, a visitor asked, "How did a man, his wife, and eleven children sleep in this small house?"

Sarah retorted to me, "That's none of his business." I replied, "Let's write about it."

In the front of the house were the furniture and the furnishings that you see on display today at the Jarrell Plantation.

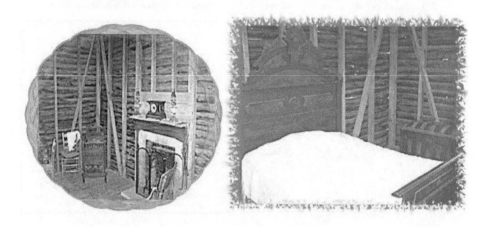

Papa and Mama slept on the double bed. Underneath the double bed was a trundle bed on which Sarah, Blake and I slept, lying cross-wise. Our arms and legs could have over-lapped at times but I cannot remember any discomfort from sleeping in this manner. We regret that we could not locate the bed and return it to the Plantation but Mama gave it away years ago. Bessie occupied the youth bed and Mildred slept in the cradle.

In the back room was a double bed. This was where Milton and Hiram slept. Allyne slept on a cot. We were unable to recall where Charlie slept. We surmise that he slept with Milton and Hiram. Papa set up a bed in the shop. Richard and Willie slept there.

So you can see that we were not bedded down like a litter of puppies.

On the wall by our parents' bed hung a sword which had belonged to Papa's Uncle Chapman Burden, who was wounded in the Civil War. Also on the wall was a portrait of Mama's brother, Uncle Frank Van Zandt, who lost his life as he served as a brakeman for the Southern Railway.

A very necessary item for the home where there were children was the chamber pot. Mama simply called it the chamber. It was several years later that I learned that the word was not an ugly word but a word that meant "room".

Between the hall and the southeast corner of the room was what you would call a dresser. We called it the bureau. In the bottom drawer were the bed linens. There were no "wash and wear" fabrics in those days. You can understand how long it took Allyne and Mama to do the ironing. In the next drawer were more linens and Papa's

clothes. There were three short drawers. In the bottom drawer were Papa's socks.

It seemed that he had more socks than anyone in the family. In the middle drawer, there were handkerchiefs. Since there were no facial tissues available in those days, there had to be an ample supply of handkerchiefs.

In the top drawer were important papers to be kept, such as bills, tax notices, obituaries cut from the local paper and other important items. Mama kept her bottle of Tutt's pills there. Also, papa kept his bag of small change in that drawer.

On the top of the bureau, near the back, was a little brownish gray ceramic container. In it one could find various articles which had no other place to be put, such as hair pins, safety pins, fine-tooth comb, button hook, et cetera. Behind it were current letters which could be read repeatedly until it was decided how to discard it. In front of the container was the family's only comb and brush.

About ten feet in front of the fireplace, suspended from the ceiling was a family treasure, a swinging lamp as we called it. In latter years, it was purloined by some visitor to the plantation.

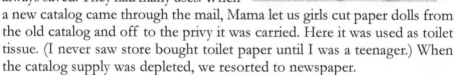

Opposite the bureau in the northeast corner of the room was a table. It was covered with a red-figured oilcloth. On the table were two lamps, a Bible, a dictionary, a Sears, Roebuck Catalog and a stack of neatly piled newspapers. Mama always referred to one lamp as "Aunt Jule's wedding present". It had a blue knobbed stem and a yellow bowl for the oil.

The catalog and the newspapers were always saved. They had many uses. When a new catalog came through the mail, Mama let us girls cut paper dolls from the old catalog and off to the privy it was carried. Here it was used as toilet tissue. (I never saw store bought toilet paper until I was a teenager.) When the catalog supply was depleted, we resorted to newspaper.

Flybrush

Remember that screens were not available at that time. When a meal was served, the greedy flies that were not already in the room, swarmed in through the open windows to get their fair share of the food. When Mama was ready to serve a meal, she called one of the children who reached to the top of the safe and took the fly brush down to shoo off the flies by waving the fly brush. People who did not own a fly brush often ran outside and broke off a limb from a nearby bush. It had the leaves intact. To make a fly brush, one procured a reed, about five feet long. Onto it were sewn two sheets of newspapers that were 3 ft. plus 2 ft. slit into 2 inch wide strips.

"Daisy Fly Killers" were set out. These were sealed metal boxes approximately four inches wide, six inches long and an inch thick. On the top was a picture of several daisies. In the center of one daisy was a wick which permitted the poisonous liquid contained within the box to be accessible to the flies.

"Tanglefoot" fly paper was also used. Six sets per box were sold, I think. Each set consisted of two papers which were stuck together with an extremely sticky substance. The papers were pulled apart and placed at places where flies gathered to look for food. They would quickly be entrapped by the sticky substance. When the  sheet had ensnared a couple hundred or more flies, it was burned.

Lamplighters were also made from newspaper. To make a lamplighter, two inch-wide strips of newspaper were cut. They were rolled into a roll. The ends were pulled out, thus forming a taper from a tightly wound spiral of paper twelve or sixteen inches long. They were placed in a vertical position in a tin can and placed on the mantel. Money was scarce and matches cost money, perhaps five cents a box. During the winter months, the lamplighters were used. When the sun went down and day turned into night, a lamplighter was ignited from the blazing fire and the tiny flame transported to the wick of the lamp. The tiny flame was extinguished and the lamplighter was placed again in the tin can on the mantel. A lamplighter lasted several nights, perhaps a week.

When the annual bee-robbing time came, paper which had been rolled in a tight bundle was ignited. The smoldering smoke repelled the bees while the men took the honey.

In the springtime when baby chicks were being hatched, a battered bucket was lined with paper to be used to transfer the biddies from the nest to the coop.

If the eggs were to be sent to the market or to a neighbor, crumbled paper ensured the eggs against breakage.

Pieces of paper were used to roll up the hair and make it curly.

On the wall between the fireplace and table hung the current calendar. Beneath it always hung the previous year's calendar. One year when the new calendar arrived, Allyne exclaimed, "It's a picture of John Paul Jones!" I thought she said "Grandpa Jones". I knew Grandpa Van Zandt and had heard that Grandpa Jarrell had been dead for many years. It was a long time before I learned that I had no Grandpa Jones.

Both Mama's and Papa's trunks were in the back room. On cold or rainy days, we played on them. They were our horses whose names were "Go Shack" and "Shackle Foot". If ever we heard Mama open her trunk, we went running to look and smell the fragrance exuded by the talcum powder that was somewhere within the trunk. We also wanted to look at Mama's few cherished possessions, especially her wedding dress. We never ran when Papa opened his trunk because there was nothing of interest in it. When he died at the age of ninety-one, I think that he had stored in his trunk every receipt that he had accumulated since he graduated from Mercer University.

Somewhere in that back room was a book entitled <u>A Child's Story of the Bible</u> . We looked at the pictures and the older siblings read the stories to us. The most impressive picture in the book was that of the drowning people. How my heart went out to them! This was the only religious instruction that I had at home. Both Mama and Papa were so busy but they strongly taught us right from wrong. Three times daily, Papa said the blessing, "Be pleased our Father. Pardon our sins and make us thankful for these and other blessing, we beg for Christ's sake. Amen." When we had "company" (the word "guest" was not in our vocabulary), Papa always added two more words in this supplication. He added "many" before the word "sins" and "humbly" before beg.

Also in the room was Papa's homemade desk with a small bookcase resting upon it. There were usually several boxes such as fruit jar boxes in which clothing and quilts were kept.

As one came up the back steps from the yard to the open hall, one would see two shelves at the top of the steps. On one shelf, there were two buckets of water. The one with the freshest water contained the dipper from which we all drank. The other bucket contained the stale water with which we washed our hands.

On the slightly lower shelf were the wash basins and may I explain that there were three kinds of soap used. When we had visitors, Mama put out the store-bought scented soap. There was the octagon soap which was used to wash hands and feet. There was the home-made lye soap used for washing dishes, scouring the floor and for washing clothes. The word "mopping" was not in vogue at that time.

In the back end of the hall were five or six shelves. They were used as a catch-all. Here were empty fruit jars, jars filled with fruit, cardboard boxes being saved for future use, paper bags and anything else that we had no place for. Once a bag of cotton was found to be the maternity ward for four baby kittens.

In the small dining room, there was a table. On one side were chairs and on the other was a long bench.

Over in the corner was an article of furniture which today's society call a "pie safe". We simply called it a "safe". On the top shelve was a stack of saucers and a stack of bowls that doubled for soup bowls or for oatmeal. There were also a bottle of vinegar, one of pepper sauce and two stemmed goblets, turned upside down, on which Mama placed a saucer

or plate of butter. There were other things which I could not see very well... Oh, yes, a box of toothpicks. Willie always kept his toothbrush there in a glass.

On the middle shelf were empty pitchers and empty bowls. Below on the bottom shelf were pitchers filled with milk and a stack of twelve or fifteen large plates.

One of the small drawers contained knives, forks and spoons. The other small drawer held the "dry cloths". They were usually sugar sacks that had been ripped open to make dish towels.

In the lower compartment were the everyday towels

which in reality were salt sacks that had been ripped open and neatly hemmed. A big box of Epsom salts was kept there, too.

In the kitchen were the stove, a table and a chopping block. The stove did not radiate enough heat to keep the dining room warm. During the cold winter months, Mama would often serve our plates and let us stand eating with our plates on the top of the stove. In the kitchen, the table was covered with neatly packed boxes and buckets. Cooking utensils were hung from the wall. The chop block was a homemade article. It had three legs attached to it. The top was well sanded and served its purpose.

NEW HOME

When the boys returned home from the armed forces we all concentrated on getting the new house finished. We children picked up flint rocks from the hillside on which the Jarrell Plantation Visitors Center is now located. They were transported to a huge six-foot high box that had been built in front of what is now Philip Haynes' home. Later they were mixed in the cement that formed the bases for the pillars of the house.

Having seen only a few people moving, I visualized that Papa would hitch up the wagon and the piled high wagon would carry everything across the road. To my surprise, we all pitched in and toted every single piece of furniture and furnishings across the road. When we had moved all but the stove, I felt surely it would take the wagon. Surprise again! The boys took 2 x 4's and placed them under it and away they went. Mildred moved the cats four or five times but they wandered back to the old house each time.

As we moved into the new house we chose or were assigned to sleeping quarters. Richard and Hiram chose the front room upstairs on the west side while Milton and Charlie shared the upstairs back room on the west side. Willie was given the back bedroom upstairs on the east side of the house. Allyne became situated in the front east side room upstairs with Bessie as her roommate and later Mildred joined them. Mama and Papa occupied the east side back bedroom downstairs, adjoining what would later be a bathroom. Since Bessie was not well, she later was given the back room on the west side of the building. The youth bed and two other beds were placed in the future bathroom adjoining our parents' room. Sarah, Mildred and I slept there.

The bathroom on the back porch later became Mildred's and my playroom. The front room on the west side was not completed. It was a long work table piled with newspapers and was a catch-all for everything. We saved the funny papers, today called the comic sections. On rainy days, we sat in that room and perused the week or month's old papers.

It was wonderful to be in a new house. Our wealth had not increased but our space had. Near the window was Mama's sewing machine. We learned early never to touch Mama's machine. When a neighbor told us about her little brother George, "George fell off the 'chine and broke his collar bone", we just could not visualize a child doing such a thing as climbing onto the machine.

When Mama used all the thread from the spool, she gave the empty spool to one of us children. If Blake received it, he could whittle it into a toy called a dancer. It had a stem through the middle of the spool and when the stem was twirled, the dancer would spin like a top. We girls usually used our spools as bubble makers. Sometimes after blowing bubbles, we passed a string through the spool and pulled it along the floor as a toy for the kittens.

RESPONSIBILITIES

As all children did, so did we all have responsibilities. My first job was to take out the chamber. How I detested the job. This entailed taking the chamber down toward the shop, emptying it, rinsing it and placing it atop a row of wooden hen nests which caught the southern sun rays. Thus the chamber was deprived of its stench and hopefully germs. In late afternoon, I would have to carry it back into the house and place it under the bed.

Stove wood was usually sawed from pine saplings and were four to six inches in diameter. The boys then with the use of the axe split them into quarters. We children then stacked them into "pig pens" to hasten the drying. We had to carry sufficient stove wood into the stove room each afternoon. The word "kitchen" was not in our vocabulary at that time.

During the winter months, heavier wood was cut for the fireplace. That wood pile was across the road directly in front of the house. At this age, I did not carry heavy wood.

Picking up wood chips and carrying in splinters were also our responsibilities. Splinters were slivers of wood cut from light wood knots, often called "light 'ood knots". These knots came from roots of the pine trees where turpentine was stored. With these splinters and a few wood chips a fire was easily kindled.

At an early age we carried water from the well using gallon buckets.

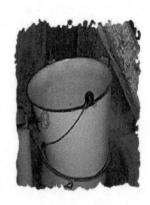

During early spring weeks, we pulled clover for the cow's dessert, thus enriching their milk. Later in the summer there were half ripe peaches or apples that had fallen to the ground. They must be removed and carried to the hogs. Sometimes there were dried peas to be picked. Always, during the spring, summer, and early fall, there were calves to be cared for. We tied a fifteen foot rope around the calf's neck and lead it, sometimes forcibly, to a grassy spot. There the calf was tied to a nearby tree to graze until noon. Then it was watered and moved to another spot to remain until night. From there it was led to the barn to spend the night after having been given more nourishment.

In addition to the duties already mention, there were blackberries to be picked. Also there was water to be carried to the fields every hour if Papa and Willie worked near the house. If they were working at a distance they carried heavy thick jugs of water that were placed in a waterhole. A waterhole was a three-foot hole dug in the shade. A jug of water stored there would keep the water cool for several hours.

One summer we had five rows of string beans. A rainy season came. It seems that all of those beans matured at the same time. Instead of working inside, I enjoyed picking the beans in the rain. Mama, Papa, and Allyne worked inside stringing the beans and canning them. Mama canned fifty one-half gallon of beans in those three days.

It was probably in 1918 that the boll weevil invaded the South. Some of the infested bolls dropped off. We children had to pick them up to be burned. At any rate Papa made very little cotton that year.

The days were long and the weather was hot but we all picked cotton. Papa gave me a nickel for picking cotton. That was the only money that I was ever paid for doing any farm work. And I lost that. I was playing with the coin and it rolled through a crack in the floor. I was scolded and of course I cried. I went under the house and found it.

SKILLS

During the first eighteen years of our lives we were learning skills that we thought would last for our lifetime. Fortunately, we find that most of these skills are outmoded.

Are you snorting in disgust learning that we changed clothes only once a week? How would you have managed to get the laundry done for eleven children with no running water, no machinery, only drudgery?

One of the children, usually Charlie, went up to the well, turned the tubs right side up, washed out the wash pot and began drawing water. When the wash pot was nearly filled with water, a fire was built beneath it so that the water could be heating and ready for Mama to begin the washing. By the time that Mama had arrived, the first tub had sufficient water in it that she could dip a gallon or two from the boiling pot and begin to wash. She placed a copious amount of **Grandma's Washing Powder** into the pot and a cake of lye soap. She began with the sheets. She had a corrugated washboard to scrub on the difficult spots. They were put on the battling board and beat with what was called a battling stick which loosened whatever dirt it could.

The sheets were then placed in the boiling pot of water. While these sheets boiled, she scrubbed on a second load. The boiled sheets were removed from the pot with the use of the battling stick, beat again and placed in the second tub where they were scrubbed again. They were rinsed in tubs number three and four. Tub number five held the bluing water. Into this water had been stirred a spoonful or more of a powder which we bought in wooden boxes. The powder was made from the indigo plant. It served the purpose of what we now call Clorox.

The sheets were then hung on the clothesline. There was a designated order in which clothes were washed. Bed linens, towels, white wearing clothes, colored wearing apparel, men's shirts, men's overalls and lastly the socks.

Mama had the most stamina of any woman I've ever known. On a cold wintry day she rode in a buggy with Papa twenty miles to Macon, had all of her teeth extracted and returned home the same day. The next day, she went up to the well and did the family wash in near freezing weather.

Tuesday was ironing day. Three irons were placed on the stove to heat. When they reached a temperature which was thought hot enough, they were tested. To test the iron for a high enough temperature, the person ironing touched her finger to her tongue, just long enough to dampen the finger. She touched the iron with her finger. If it sizzled, then it was hot enough. As the temperature of irons waned they were rotated on the stove. After each garment was ironed, it was carefully folded and placed in a neat pile for whatever place it was to be stored. The starched pieces had been previously sprinkled and wrapped in a towel. They were the last articles to be ironed.

At the age of ten, Allyne taught me to milk. Many people think that a yank on the teat brings milk. Not so! I was instructed to place my hand on the side of teat, press down with the index finger, then the second finger and finely the pinky. If done in a quick succession, a stream of milk will come out. After mastering the procedure with the right hand, the left hand could be done. Soon one can sit on a stool and milk with both hands simultaneously.

Few people under fifty years of age can understand why anyone could or would want buttermilk. People in the country would have two options: 1) They could drink sweet milk and have no butter, or; 2) They could drink buttermilk and have butter. Most people chose the latter.

Each family had two or more churns. When the cows were milked at night, milk for the children and the morning coffee was set aside. The remainder was poured into a churn. The next morning and night, the procedure was the same. Within twenty-four or thirty-six hours the milk had "turned". By that expression, it meant that the milk had soured and turned into a thick mass called clabber.

To test the turning of the milk, Mama tilted the churn on its side. One could see that the mass did not cling to the churn and appeared to be thick. While Mama cooked breakfast, Papa churned. The dasher shaft was put through the hole in the lid and then into the churn. Papa, or someone designated, plunged the dasher up and down for a period of probably forty minutes or until globules of fat or butter separated from the milk and had risen to the top of the milk. The dasher was swirled around until the butter formed in a mass. The butter was taken up by the aid of the butter paddle. The butter was washed and all of the buttermilk was excreted out. Any experienced housewife knew how much salt was needed for the amount of butter produced. It was smoothed over and some attractive design was imprinted with the butter paddle as the mass of butter was placed on a saucer or butter dish.

During the warm months, Mama filled a gallon milk can that had a close-fitting lid and a bail. Each of us would take milk to the spring and would hang it by its bail to a strip of wood stretching across the spring. At noon time we would hurry down and bring the good cool buttermilk to be served with our dinner. Sometimes on the way to and from the fields, Papa would take it. After we had finished eating, Mama filled the can from a pitcher of buttermilk sitting in the safe. Of course, the process was repeated at supper time.

Raising sweet potatoes was one of Papa's specialties. In this, we children helped a great deal. Papa planned and planted the potato bed. These young plants were called "slips". When potato planting time came around, Papa went down to the spring where they were bedded. He selected a handful of slips. It is amazing how he could ascertain how many slips were needed for any piece of land. He went along with the hoe and dug holes two or three inches deep, and eight or ten inches apart. One of us went along behind him and poured a dipper or more of water into the hole, according to the moisture that was already present in the soil. Another one of us dropped a slip in each hole. Then one of us either stooped or squatted down to plant the slip by pulling soil down around it. Of course, we rotated or helped each other plant the slips. When no rain came, it was necessary to water the plants for several days.

After several weeks, the potato plants had grown four feet long. It was time for Willie to plow the potatoes. We would have to turn the vines so that they could be plowed. That was all of the cultivation that was necessary.

In late October or early November, before a hard freeze came, the potatoes had to be dug. Our job was to pick up the potatoes and place them in the wagon. I don't know how many loads of potatoes there were…but several. The potatoes were unloaded down the bank in front of the 1920 house. There were five or six holes, six feet in diameter and perhaps sixteen inches deep. These holes were lined with several inches of pine straw. We all, including Mama, graded the potatoes. We wished to get them all graded by nightfall. Their categories were: cut potatoes, which would be the first that we eat; seed potatoes and the rest would be graded according to their size. They were then covered with a thick layer of pine straw, a layer of dirt and boards atop all of this.

Another skill we learned was making syrup. In the spring of the year, cane was planted. To plant cane, no seeds were actually planted. The entire stalk of cane was laid horizontally on the ground and was covered with several inches of dirt. Between each joint of cane there was a bud which sprouted. It grew and the cane was cultivated as any other crop. In the fall, the cane stalks were cut down and the fodder removed. The stalks were them moved to the site of the cane mill. That is, all but those stalks that had been selected for seed. The seed cane did not have its fodder removed. It was piled horizontally on the ground and covered with dirt to await the planting time next spring.

I cannot understand why people said "cane grinding". The cane was not ground. It was pressed between two huge rollers which pressed the stalks. The only time that I remember helping with this chore, Papa was short of help. Willie tended feeding the boiler and operating the engine that operated the cane mill. Sarah fed the mill and I moved the cane mashes from the mill. Aunt Matt tended the fire under the evaporator while Papa and Mama and Aunt Julie tended the cooking of the juice into syrup. I don't know where Allyne was.

The cane mill was operated spasmodically. Only a few minutes were needed to fill a tub with juice.

It took quite some time for enough juice to evaporate before adding more to the evaporator. When the work was nearly done, Mama was excused to go home. Aunt Matt relinquished her job and Papa finished the cooking and filling of the many containers. Sarah, Mildred and I lugged them up to the smokehouse where they were stored. It took quite some time for us to get them up the hill. We had had an enjoyable time making the syrup and we had an enjoyable time eating hot buttered biscuits with fresh syrup that night.

Butchering hogs was another day-long job. We did not call it "butchering". We said "hog-killing". Older people often referred to intensely cold weather as "hog-killing" weather. The doomed hogs were shot with a .22 rifle with the bullet being inflicted between the eyes. The throats were slit and allowed to bleed. Then the hogs were immediately scalded, their hair scraped off, cut open and dressed. We children took no part in this. That night, we enjoyed eating fresh meat.

On the next day we had no specific chore but helped wherever we were needed. On that day sausage meat was cut, ground and seasoned. Lard was rendered. Mama's huge black pot was placed in the fireplace of the kitchen. All of the fat that had been cut from the hog was place in the pot. As it cooked, the oil was rendered from the fat. The substance skimmed off was "cracklings". The cracklings were used to season cornbread and thus called crackling bread. Some called it shortening bread. Making sausage and rendering lard was all done at the same time.

We girls helped as needed. Sometimes, we stirred the lard; other times we turned the crank to grind the sausage meat. Sometimes we washed dishes. Other times, we ran errands as needed. Aunt Julie helped with all of this procedure.

Springtime came. On alternate years, our apple trees produced an abundance of fruit. We picked up fruit as it fell to the ground. I think that Papa peeled more apples than anyone else. If any apples were canned, the peelings and cores were cooked into jelly.

Many apples were dried. To dry apples, slices of apples were placed on a board which was then placed in the hot sunshine. Of course, the skies were constantly watched for impending frequent showers that often came up. After a few days in the hot summer sun, the apples had shriveled enough to be placed on smaller boards. When the apples were pronounced cured, they were place in a flour sack and tied at the neck of the sack. During the fall and winter months, the apples were often placed out in the sun to prevent mold from developing. They were used to make apple puffs (sometimes called apple tarts), apple pies, and sometimes applesauce. Dried apples were used a couple of years until another crop was produced.

There were several peach trees that produced enough peaches to have canned peaches and some peach preserves. Figs were plentiful and Mama made many cans of fig preserves.

Every child learned to make house brooms from broom sedge, although most people called it "broom sage". This plant grew and still grows in open fields where the ground lies fallow. Most housewives tried to gather plants that were five feet tall or taller. The stalks were cleaned by using an old fork to remove the excess leaves from the stem of the plant. A handful of the broom sedge was gathered together. A heavy cord was wound around it holding it together.

Brush brooms, also called yard brooms, were made. They were often made from dogwood limbs. They were used to sweep trash from yards that seldom had grass growing on it.

Yes, we learned to sharpen axes while turning the grindstone. In like manner, we pumped the bellows at the blacksmith shop, watching the plowshares being sharpened on the anvil. Boys learned to grease the buggy axles and to shoe mules.

There were two engine holes that furnished water for the boiler to make steam to operate the machinery. One of them had very steep sides and was very deep. One day, one of the yearling calves came down for a drink of water. We heard a plunk and saw the calf floundering in the water. We understood that he could not get out of the water and we knew that we could not help him. We knew that Richard was working up at the shop. We all ran up there yelling hysterically. Richard came down. He reached down and grasped an ear with each hand and pulled the calf to safety. I felt so sorry for the poor little calf.

We learned how corn was ground, how logs were sawed into timber, how wheat was threshed and how hay was harvested.

In those days, the beds had to be made daily. We did not have mattresses as we have today. Our beds were more like huge bags of cotton. Each day, it was fluffed and turned over. The sheets and quilts were placed on it.

Needle work was learned much as it is learned today.

As Papa grew older and some of the children left home, he seemed to grow more mellow. He taught me to hunt squirrels. We took Snooks, the little fox terrier, with us. Snooks picked up the trail and followed it until it ended at a tree. There we found the squirrel high in the tree. When the squirrel saw us, it would go to the opposite side of the tree. Here's where my part of the work was done. I went to the side where the squirrel was hiding. He hastened to the side on which Papa was standing with the gun. BANG! We had the squirrel. You are sympathizing with the squirrel, I know. There was an epidemic of squirrels that year. They were destroying the corn crop and also the pecan crop of unripened pecans. If the livestock were to eat and if we were to have cornbread, we had to rid ourselves of the squirrels and produce meat for our tables.

One year there was an epidemic of ticks that was plaguing the cows. I do not know who spearheaded the situation but dipping vats were dug in various parts of the county. A dipping vat was a long trench, perhaps thirty feet or more in length and was a trifle wider than the fattest cow. Its depth was approximately five or perhaps six feet. On each side was a wooden fence which was high enough to deter a dissatisfied cow from jumping out. The vat was filled with water that was medicated with a tick-killing solution. At the entrance end of the vat was a pen that held a man's entire herd of cattle. One cow at a time was driven into the steep end of the vat. When it was half-way through the journey through the vat, a man with a long pole soused the cow's head under the water to ensure that all of the ticks would be doused. The cow continued her journey and up the ramp at the end of the vat to be enclosed in a pen to await her comrades and to be herded on toward home.

This cow-dipping was held on alternate weeks. I can remember it for one reason.

When returning from the vat one day, one of Aunt Matt's cows named Pearl, decided that enough was enough. She darted around the gate of the cowpen and headed for who knows where. She saw three-year old Mildred and charged toward her. Eleven year old Bessie saw the situation. She ran toward the irate cow waving a broom, thus saving Mildred from being badly injured or killed. A Guardian Angel watched over us in those days.

Robbing bees was another annual activity. Papa had five or six gums as we called them. Today they are referred to as hives. In early years, they were called gums because they were made of sweet gum. I was told this but I am not sure that that statement is authentic.

At one time during these early years a very disgraceful event transpired. We became infested with bedbugs! For several days each week and for several weeks the entire family labored to rid ourselves of this pest. Every morning the mattresses were "looked". They were then carried out into the hot sunshine and left until late afternoon. The furniture was wiped with a cloth that had been saturated with kerosene. The crevices were scalded. After a few weeks we felt we were safe.

FUN THINGS

Too, there were fun things for us to do. When the sawmill wasn't in operation we played on the sawdust pile. Blake devised many games. Nearby the saw dust pile, there was a stream. With mud and debris, we fashioned a dam across the stream so that we would have deeper water in which to wade.

One day Sarah and Blake fished out a snake and killed it. I watched. I am sure that it was a moccasin. Our Guardian Angel was protecting us again.

Papa rigged up some kind of conveyance to carry the slabs away from the sawmill. He called this contraption "the dummy". Charlie, who was about twelve years old like to ride on it. We were entrusted to his care to ride on it. We spent some happy afternoons.

There is a rather steep hill between Aunt Matt's house and the gin house. It was covered with pine straw. Of course, it afforded a wonderful place for us to play. We each found a stave of a barrel. It became a sled. That hill became the place for long hours of amusement. Had we ever seen skiing or even heard about skiing, I am sure that we would have attempted to ski on our sliding boards.

Where there were saplings less than twenty feet tall we would bend over, get astride them and pretend that they were horses as we bounced and trounced on them. After riding our horses we climbed twenty or more feet up the tree and swayed in the tree tops. Again Guarding Angels watched over us and prevented us from falling and breaking our necks.

When Mildred was born, people said, "You aren't the baby any longer." I had never thought of myself as a baby. I was so surprised.

Mildred did not grow as a newly-born baby should have. Mama was so thin. A neighboring lady gave birth to a lively son in the same week that Mama gave birth to Mildred. Sally had a voluptuous bosom that produced an ultra amount of nourishment. She came up twice daily and nursed Mildred.

I felt that Mildred did not grow fast enough to satisfy me. I did not realize that she was just different from me. She did not enjoy running, jumping or any competitive games.

Once I tried to entice Mildred to go into the woods, carrying her dolls, and have a picnic. She vehemently said, "No!" When I asked her why, she replied that she was afraid a boa constrictor would get her. Of course, I derided her. After she had celebrated her eighteenth birthday, she sent me a picture clipped from the Dublin paper. A man from Wrightsville was holding a boa constrictor which had been discovered nearby. Mildred had written on the picture, "I told you so!"

Mildred and I played together nicely most of the time with our shoe boxes of paper dolls. Sometimes we forgot and left them outside our playroom.

Sarah would find them and dispose of them, usually burning them. In that case, we had to wait an eternity before accumulating another box full.

On several occasions, jealousy or some Satanic Power took possession of me. I think that it was the latter. I would kidnap Mildred's favorite doll and hold her for a ransom. The ransom was that she would carry in my share of stove wood or to take my rambunctious calf to water.

When Mildred was about three years old we decided to take her on an expedition. We went out on the ridge beyond where the washhouse is now located. We crawled under the fence and soon located a glorious red clay gully. We older children could run up and down the sides of the gully. Mildred's short legs prohibited her from doing as we did.

She slid on her little behind. After having had a superb time, we went home. It didn't take long for Mama to discover Mildred's little red drawers. Was she angry! She didn't punish us but we never took Mildred on another or our jaunts.

One day, having nothing to do, we went up into the barn and opened the shutter. Someone suggested having a spitting contest. Blake won.

In later years, when springtime came, so did jump-rope season come. No home could spare a rope for the children to jump. A rope was a precious commodity. Well, what did we use for a jump-rope? Very simple, a muscadine vine would suffice. In those days all boys carried a pocket knife at all times.

No one would become irate that he would think of inflicting a wound on someone else. I cannot recall seeing or hearing of even a fist fight during my early school days. Either some girls borrowed a pocket knife or some boys went with the girls into the nearby woods, found a 12 foot or longer muscadine vine, cut it from the mother plant, and brought it to school. There it was trimmed of branches and twigs.

Two girls, one on either end of the rope, held the ends. As they turned the rope, various girls would run in and jump. The games varied. Sometimes, one would be assigned "hot peas". This would involve the rope being turned very fast. The speed would be increased to see just how fast one could jump. At another time, one would jump "high waters". That was letting the rope come within several inches of striking the ground. When the would-be jumper hesitated before running into the rope to jump, she was said to be "swallowing gnats". At times, two girls would play "chasing the fox". One girl ran in beside the rope-turner A, jumped the rope once or twice however having been agreed upon and run out on the opposite side, and around rope-turner B, and back into the jump-rope with the second girl chasing her.

Another game was for two girls to enter simultaneously from opposite ends of the rope. After meeting in the middle, they exited at the opposite ends. This was called "crossing the river". "Going in the back door" meant exactly what it said. One entered from the opposite side of the rope.

Then there was "going under the moon". Here the jumper ran through the rope without jumping or being touched by the rope.

Whenever a girl missed a jump, she assumed the task of being a rope turner.

Older girls often played "Mumblepeg". (Small children were not allowed to play this game because of the danger involved.) A group of three or four girls sat around a pile of dirt. An open knife was thrown in a manner in which the blade of the knife entered into the dirt with the knife pointed downward and the knife assumed a vertical position.

There were various angles at which it was thrown. The game never appealed to me. I never learned to play the game.

When marbles were available, the boys shot marbles. I was never interested in that game because I could never learn to shoot the marbles. When the boys had no marbles, they often found white clay in some remote place. A sufficient number was rolled out and placed in the hot sun where they soon dried.

We had no toys but we could improvise. I never had a doll until I was twelve years old when my sister bought a used doll from a friend of hers. To make a doll, I found the end of a pine bough that looked like Drawing A. I broke it off at point x and removed the Pine needles as shown in Drawing B. Can you see how imaginative we were?

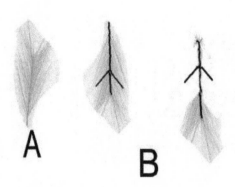

Not having a tea set, I went to the clay bank and molded dinnerware which was set in the sun to harden. Leaves and grass became our vegetables, i.e. tiny rocks made excellent peas.

During the summer months we often fashioned animals and articles from maypops. Today's children refer to them as the fruits of the passion flower.

Moving into the community to work in the sawmill industry was Rich and Clara McGee with their three-year old Margaret and ten-year old, Robert. Rich had an often repeated expression…"A poor man has a hard time."

Robert and I played peacefully together. Many, many times he was at our house just as dinner was being served. Mama always asked him to eat. Robert, a normal hungry boy, always accepted the invitation. Mama was favorably impressed with him. Unfailingly when he finished his meal, he always said, "Mrs. Jarrell, I sure enjoyed my dinner." No other child showed that much appreciation without a parent prompting him.

PEOPLE, PLACES AND THINGS

FOOD

Since there were no neighborhood stores in which to buy commodities and since money was almost non-existent, we had to do with what we had. When Papa made his semi-annual trip to Macon, he usually bought several huge boxes of oatmeal, sugar, salt and coffee.

For breakfast, we always had oatmeal. During spring and summer when they were plentiful, we had eggs each day. Of course, Mama cooked huge pans of biscuits for her eleven children. Once or perhaps twice each week, we had some form of fried meat for breakfast, i.e. chicken, ham, shoulder, streak of lean, fish or canned sausage.

During the spring, summer and early fall, we had an abundance of fresh vegetables. Many times we would have chicken pie or chicken and dumplings for dinner and supper. With all of her work, Mama cooked only two meals each day. That which was left over from dinner was served warmed over for supper. During the winter months, there were turnips, turnip greens, collards, mustard greens and an abundance of dried black-eyed peas and dried butterbeans. On Sundays, Mama always opened a half gallon of canned string beans...we always called them snap beans. With an abundance of canned blackberries, canned peaches and dried apples, desserts were not a problem except for the sugar. Often during the week, Mama made a syrup pudding. Of course with sweet potatoes in abundance, there were sweet potato desserts.

CLOTHING

For summer wear, my clothes consisted of a drawers waist, drawers, an underskirt on cool days and an apron. The drawers waist was a sleeveless bodice opening in the back with four buttons fastening it in the back. There was a button on each side and one in front with which the drawers were fastened to the drawers waist at the bottom on each side. The drawers were like pants. They were made of a flour sack. Mama had washed it with lye soap, and had boiled it until it was white. Some of my friends had drawers with pictures on them or print because their mothers failed to wash it as thoroughly as Mama had. I never heard of the "slip" until I was a teenager. The underskirt was a garment with a skirt gathered onto a bodice. The underskirt worn in the winter was usually made of grey flannel. The apron was a very plain garment opening down the back with a high neck line and with long sleeves. We had two of the aprons. They were worn for a week. On Saturday afternoon, we had a bath and changed to clean clothes. In winter time, we wore a union suit under the other clothes. Our winter drawers were made of cotton flannel. The union suit was what is now called "Long Johns". In winter, we wore black stockings held up by garters which we called elastics. Oh how the Achilles tendons and the chapped heels hurt as they cracked open by the cold weather. The black lint would get into our cracked skin. Tallow was applied each night but the next day there would be a repetition of cracked skin. When I read of Washington's men spending the winter at

Valley Forge and how their feet became so cold, I empathized with them. We wore high-topped shoes with eight or ten buttons on each shoe. A button hook was used to button them.

When girls became a little older and hips had developed, they no longer wore drawers waists but drawers were buttoned as skirts are buttoned today. The older girls sometimes wore laced shoes but still wore union suits.

The boys' underdrawers were made of heavier material than that of the girls. Their shirts were made of Hickory Shirting. All of the winter underwear and the overalls were ordered from Sears.

Bessie and Sarah were practically the same size although Bessie was two years older. Neither girl had a Sunday dress. A relative sent her daughter's outgrown dress to Mama. The dress was a good fit on both girls. Who should possess the dress? Mama solved the problem beautifully. Bessie would wear the dress on one occasion while Sarah stayed at home. The next time Sarah would wear the dress and Bessie stayed home.

I understand that one fall, Papa drew around each of our feet, went to town and bought twenty pairs of shoes. The shoes were for eleven of us children, four cousins at Aunt Matt's, Aunt Matt, and a pair for him and one for Mama. I do not know for whom were the other two pairs unless it was for a couple of field hands.

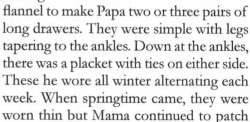

Each fall, Mama bought enough cotton flannel to make Papa two or three pairs of long drawers. They were simple with legs tapering to the ankles. Down at the ankles, there was a placket with ties on either side. These he wore all winter alternating each week. When springtime came, they were worn thin but Mama continued to patch them and they lasted until the next fall.

In Papa's drawer of the bureau were a couple of white shirts which were kept washed and starched for dress wear. It was stylish in those days for men to wear detachable collars which were starched as stiff as a board. Mama laboriously washed, starched and ironed them after each use. This was about once each month. Church services were held on the fourth Saturday and Sunday of each month.

BAREFOOT

In early springtime, all children looked forward to going barefoot. Mama was the last woman in Jones County to let her little ones go barefoot lest they would take cold. Even when she decided to let us go barefoot, it was nearly ten o'clock before she deemed it warm enough. One day, I removed my shoes, my old black stockings and elastics. I folded the stockings neatly and placed the elastics on top of them making sure that they were out of the way of anyone and on the back porch. The elastics were looped together lest one get lost. The next day I was required to wear the shoes until the day had warmed sufficiently. As I began to put on the stocking, I saw that my looped together elastics were nowhere to be seen. Mama reprimanded me by saying that if I had placed them where they should have been placed they would have been there. I was adamant. No one believed me. A few minutes later we heard a nauseated dog in the backyard. He regurgitated the elastics, still looped together.

MEDICINE

When springtime came, Mama said it was time to take medicine to work the liver. At night we were given a calomel tablet. We were warned neither to get wet nor to eat certain foods or we would become salivated.

I never knew what being salivated entailed except that the teeth would fall out. The next morning we had to take a dose of Epsom salts. That was an awful dose! Papa often took a dose as a laxative. We just couldn't understand how he did it! When we developed a cough, we were given two drops of turpentine on a teaspoon of sugar. For chest colds, we were subjected to a mustard plaster. To make a mustard plaster, something like this was concocted. A spoonful of flour was mixed with a spoonful of powdered mustard. A few drops of turpentine were added and some form of grease was added.

This was placed on a large scrap of cloth, folded over, heated over the lamp and applied to the affected chest. Time was taken to inspect the chest from time to time to see that the chest did not blister.

Mama gave Tutt's pills occasionally but I do not remember for what reason.

She had nothing to give for dry skin. She saved the tallow or fat from beef. When it cooled, it was balm for dry skin. It was better than nothing but did not heal the chapped skin. Hiram was applying a small piece of tallow to his chapped thumb. I thought it was a piece of candy. I yelled, "Give me a bite." He did. I always remembered the taste of that tallow.

Usually in the springtime, parents gave a tonic for purifying the blood. Papa gathered tag alder leaves and bark. This was boiled. The resulting tea was given. Some of my friends partook of sassafras tea or catnip tea.

For acute pain, paregoric was given. Today this drug is difficult to procure even with a prescription. I have been told that it contains opium.

I have a vague memory of Allyne and some other adult talking about a new drug called "aspirin". It would cure pain, especially headaches. They were discussing the morality of taking the drug. Hadn't God given pain to let one know that the body had been injured? Was it not blasphemy to take this new drug called "aspirin"?

CHILDHOOD ACCIDENTS

Sometimes in my earlier days, before I was old enough to attend school, a painful event occurred. I was playing beneath a peach tree which grew just outside the back window. I spied one of the prettiest insects that I had ever seen. It was a beautiful red-orange one. I just knew that it would be lovely to play with it. It was scurrying along but I eventually caught it. It either   bit or stung me. It produced a pain that I had not experienced before. I ran to Mama who was ironing, so it must have been on a Tuesday. She was humming but immediately with hardly a glance, procured a bottle of turpentine from the mantel and poured a few drops on the painful spot. Later I saw another one of these insects. I called Blake. He said that it was a cow-killer. When I later saw the picture of one, it was labeled "velvet ant". This I know now to be a member of the wasp family.

Charlie had a goat and a studebaker goat wagon. It was Charlie's prized possession. The other small members of the family felt that the goat was partly theirs also. Not me… I didn't admire that goat one bit. I simply detested him because he had butted me down one day.

One day in late fall a few days after syrup making, Billy died. He had partaken of the syrup skimmings. I joined the others in weeping.

I suffered several minor accidents. One day, as I was running around the barn, I approached an old rusty container of the chickens' drinking water. I attempted to jump over it. My foot was scraped by the old pot and a nail got stuck in my foot. I cried. It hurt. I was, however, concerned most about a new disease which I had heard about …lockjaw. I could visualize my jaws clamping shut like a vise and I would slowly and painfully starve to death. Papa had no sympathy. He said, "If you hadn't been stumbling around like an old blind mule, it would not have happened."

At another time, I climbed a peach tree which grew near the chicken house. A very heavy clothesline…almost cable size, passed through the tree. I wondered if I could sit upon it and swing. I gave it a try. I swung myself to the ground which was at least four feet below. I saw stars when I hit the ground. How my head and back did hurt! I lay there for several minutes. I knew not to tell anyone about it. If Papa learned of it, I certainly would get nothing but a scolding.

While eating a peach, the seed slipped down my throat. Sarah and Blake ran to tell Mama who immediately consulted her medical book to learn how to promote elimination. She immediately restricted me to the use of the chamber until the seed passed. Sarah predicted that the seed would sprout and a tree would come up my throat and through my mouth. Blake also had a drastic imagination. He said that Mama would cut me open and sew on buttons, and make some buttonholes. In that way she could easily find the lost peach seed and should I swallow another, there would be no trouble finding it. I thought that I liked Blake's suggestions better. Within a few days, the peach seed was eliminated.

While standing near the smokehouse, I heard Charlie and Sarah in a heated conversation. It sounded interesting. With childish curiosity, I set out to investigate. A thought occurred to me. Can I go around there with my eyes closed? I closed my eyes and set out. I didn't get far.

I tumbled down the embankment and cut a deep gash over my left eye. For once I was not scolded, although I don't remember getting any sympathy. It bled profusely and Mama wouldn't let me go to sleep because the <u>Medical Advisor</u> forbade it.

One year we had one of our few ice storms. I wanted to go outside and walk on the ice as the others did. At last, Mama gave in and let me go. I got as far as the smokehouse when my feet slipped from under me…another barrel of tears. Someone helped me to my feet but I never wanted to walk on ice again.

DEATH

If at any time there were an opportunity to go anywhere whether it promised to be boring or not, we wanted to go. One day we went to the cemetery. It was the unveiling of a monument on a grave. The Woodmen of the World were the participants. Blake and I had obtained permission to go.

While coming home from school the following Thursday, Blake complained of feeling bad and had a sore throat. When he reached home he was quite sick. Mama thought it was a bad case of sore throat and began treating it with the usual medication. When morning came, Blake was much worse. Dr. Smith was summoned. When we returned home from school that afternoon we were not allowed to enter the house but were instructed to go to Aunt Matt's house where Mildred had already been sent. **Diphtheria!** Dr. Smith gave us some kind of shot in the tummy that night. Blake died.

I do not know how the coffin was ordered but I believe that it was by telegraph from Dames Ferry and I think that it was sent up on the afternoon train. The boys, as my big brothers were called, brought it home on the wagon. That night, Mama and Aunt Matt bathed and dressed Blake and laid him in the coffin. In those days, country people did not have the services of funeral homes.

Few people had automobiles back then. Uncle Dick Burden carried Papa, Mama, Allyne and Mildred in their car. I do not know with whom Bessie, Sarah and I rode. For some reason, that person could not transport us home. Papa told us that we could ride home in the wagon that had been the hearse. The boys had ridden in it with the corpse en route to the meeting house. I developed a most severe headache. It seemed that as the wagon wheels hit each rut, my head would split open. I was crying bitterly. Bessie tried to console me by telling me that she would do my evening chores when we reached home.

Someone had made a delicious meal or rather was preparing a delicious meal of chicken and dumplings. For once in my life, I was not hungry. The meal was served at Aunt Matt's. After the older people had eaten, the second table was prepared. It was then that Bessie told Mama that I had a headache and did not want to eat. Immediately, Aunt Matt produced her flashlight which was a new invention at that time. The light disclosed a white spot in my throat. My parents knew instantly that it was diphtheria. Richard and Milton were dispatched to summon the doctor living seven miles away. They rode a mule. Willie picked me up and carried me down to our house. It was a comforting feeling to be in the arms of my favorite brother at that time and I was going home. When Richard and Milton reached the doctor's home, the doctor immediately left in his T-Model car for Macon. When Dr. Smith reached Macon, all of the drug stores were closed.

The doctor knew a druggist to call. He then procured the drugs needed and reached our house at 1:30 a.m. Between Mama, Papa and Aunt Matt, I was nursed back to health. I presume that Annie Florence, Ida Belle and Allyne carried on the cooking and caring for the others up at Aunt Matt's house.

When I was ten years old, on a beautiful cloudless October day, Bessie passed away. She had had rheumatic fever for several years but seemed to be feeling fairly well for the preceding week. Mrs. Susie Coulter was noted for making her appearance when the Death Angel passed over a house. She came to help "lay out" the corpse. This duty was usually performed by a family member and an experienced neighbor.

As I have mentioned, country people did not have funeral homes. I really do not know whether there were any funeral homes that performed that service. That night a wake was held. A few neighbors came and stayed up all night with the family. J.T. Coulter was tending the fire. He started to the woodpile to get more wood, not knowing that there were no steps from the side porch to the ground. He just stepped off. Fortunately, he was not injured.

While on the subject of funerals, I must tell about a wake a friend of mine attended. Every mirror in the house was turned toward the wall. She never learned why.

VICTORIAN IDEAS

I cannot recall Mama telling us about her mother but she evidently had many Victorian ideas. There were some plain everyday words that were forbidden to be used. There were expressions that she herself used that showed her ideas. If she were going to the toilet she would say, "I am going to the garden." We knew where she was going because the privy was located in the garden.

We were admonished never to say "bull" but say "male cow". She never said "legs" but used the term "lower limbs". "Belly" was not a word to be used. Aunt Matt enlightened us, but not in Mama's presence, that "belly" was a perfectly good word to use. It meant the entire front of the body from the stomach through the abdomen. She said that it was correct and in good taste to say, "The dog lay on his belly."

Too, the phrases "in a family way" and "in delicate health" were phrases used instead of the word "pregnant".

FEMININE MATTERS

Why people, especially mothers, were so secretive about feminine development is a profound mystery to me. After conversing with my acquaintances today, I have found that very few of them, if any, knew anything at all about menstruation until they had experienced it.

A friend of mine told that she was physically active, and it was between the ages of ten and fourteen that her mother told her that she must quit turning somersaults and cartwheels and skinning the cat, or she would break a blood vessel. On the onset of her first menstrual cycle, she ran hysterically to her mother yelling, "I've busted a blood vessel! I've busted a blood vessel!"

Young people today do not know how blessed they are for feminine products that are manufactured today. What I am about to tell is true but revolting. Before the advent of Kotex and other disposable products, women used rags, usually white ones. Neither sheets nor white cloths were ever destroyed. Girls were instructed in folding them and fitting them to their bodies. No family had cloths enough to throw any away. They were soaked in cold water, washed in hot water, boiled, dried and put away for the next menstrual period.

FIRSTS

There were several "firsts" in my life. The first dress that I made was between 1925 and 1930. I purchased three yards of fabric at ten cents per yard, a spool of thread for a nickel and a pattern for ten cents. This brought the price of my dress to less than fifty cents.

The first time I felt electricity was years before that. A thunder cloud was sounding in the background. Blake, Charlie and Sarah were present. When Charlie asked me if I wanted to feel electricity, I hesitated. Seeing my hesitancy, Charlie added, "I'll twist this short piece of wire around the wire fence and it will not be as strong." I believed him. I felt the electricity.

Once again, our guarding angel was with us.

For a long time, I had wanted to wear overalls. Papa strongly felt that the Bible forbade a woman wearing men's clothing. While Willie went to the government hospital, Papa had no one to help him farm. I bargained (the first and only time I bargained with Papa) that I would help him with the farm work if I could wear overalls. He assented. I helped by planting corn, velvet beans and peas. I learned to hoe and did almost everything except plow.

The majority of children become frustrated at their siblings at times and threaten to run away from home. I was no exception. I was actually running away! To where? I do not know. I had not planned that far in advance. When I reached the back end of the barn, my eyes detected something attached to the barn. I squatted down to scrutinize it closely. It wiggled. Forgetting my animosity toward Sarah, I ran back to the house. Papa was interested in my unique discovery. We all hurried back to the barn. Papa looked down and at once pronounced almost immediately, "Why, it's only a baby bat!"

The first and only time that I saw Gypsies was when I was about six years old. There were wagons and wagon loads of dirty piled-up belongings. For once in his long years of service, our faithful old horse snorted and tried to turn toward home. The paper stated they were congregating to have their annual burial ceremony. Papa and other farmers made sure that all livestock were securely fastened in that night, there being the rumor that all Gypsies were thieves. Not one neighbor reported anything missing.

Another first was finding ourselves infested with head lice. Allyne's friend, Mary, was visiting us. Of course, we wanted to make a good impression on her. Willie had taken Papa, Mama and Mildred over to Taylor County to visit Mama's cousin. I think it was a re-acquaintance meeting for Mama and Cousin Sallie. Around three days after the visiting party came home; Sarah complained that her head was itching. Mary said, "Lean over and let's see if you have any cooties." Sarah leaned over, placing her head in Mary's lap.

There were thousands or perhaps millions of the little creatures running hither and thither. I was then examined. Same story. Mildred underwent a crucial examination. I think that she had even more than Sarah and I had. We wondered just how many kinsmen she had infected on her trip. Allyne and Mary began to discuss how to eradicate the vermin. Since they didn't have any medications or any means to get it, they concluded that anointing our head with kerosene would be the best solution. Sarah, Mildred and I were promptly medicated.

Another first for me was the introduction to wieners and a wiener roast. When I was fourteen years old and in the eighth grade, I had never tasted a wiener. The algebra teacher promised that all students who made an A in algebra for the whole year would be honored with a wiener roast. I happened to be the only student who attained that goal. I spent the night with Sara Souther. I walked from Sara's home to the park where Miss Akin and I roasted wieners. How good they tasted!

Willie took Mama and me down to Abbeville to visit her Aunt Annie VanZandt. We stayed overnight. On the way home, we drove through Macon. Willie stopped on Second Street in front of a store named "Cash and Carry". Mama handed me a dime and instructed me to go in and buy a loaf of bread. I entered the store. People were scurrying around in the store. No one came to wait upon me. I stood bewildered. A kind and understanding man told me that I must pick a basket from the pile near the door, get my purchase and carry it to the cashier.

Bessie had made a trip to Macon via train. She had revealed the wonders of that magical city. My first trip to town was quite different. I was seven years old and I had a badly inflamed eye. Papa felt that it was quite necessary for an occultist be consulted. We arose, ate breakfast and were on our way by daybreak.

When we arrived in Macon hours later, Papa had to find a place for the mule and buggy, and locate an occultist. The specialist found no foreign object in the eye. He said that there had been something but it was gone now. After giving us medication for the eye, we departed for home. It was afternoon by then. After getting out of town and out of traffic, we ate our lunch which consisted of scrambled eggs and biscuit, jelly or jam and biscuit, ham and biscuit, and a sweet potato.

It was dark when we reached home. I had not seen or experienced the marvels that I had anticipated. It's strange that the most impressive thing that I still remember were the odors that filled the air. Even today when I smell cigar smoke, I think of that twenty-two mile trip to Macon.

COUNTING

From time to time, Mama used hired help. When she used hired help, she would hire a lady named Mamie. Miss Mamie usually brought her children with her. We were always delighted for they were such amiable playmates. We especially liked the way in which they counted when playing "Hide and Seek".

Ten, ten double ten
Forty-five fifteen,
All hid?
We and the weaver
Cat's got a fever
Pitch him in the river
To cool his fever.
All hid?
I had a little dog and his name was Rover.
When he died, he died all over.
All hid?
I went up the road and the road was muddy.
I stumped my toe and my toe got bloody.
All hid?
Old blue hen flew in the garden.
Shall we shoot her? NO, NO.
I went to the river and couldn't get across.
I jumped on my broomstick.
I thought it was a horse.
Fly in the buttermilk.
Who's gonna drink it?

There were many more lines that I've forgotten. Even these are probably not in the correct order.

There was another lady who worked for Aunt Matt who had children. They, too, had unique ways of expression themselves. We also enjoyed playing with them. I remember one of the girls telling of a story about some of their friends playing with an axe. That person playing with the axe missed the stick and cut off three of her little sister's fingers. When relating and demonstrating the incident to us, she used this very interesting way of describing it. "She cut this one nearly off. She cut this one clean off and she cut this one slap off."

In describing the stages of prevailing darkness, these girls had three expressions. "First dark" was the time after sundown but when it was still light. "Plum dark" was the stage which was dark enough to need a lantern but there were glimmers of light. "Slap dark" meant total darkness.

We not only enjoyed their company, but their ways of expressing things.

SENSITIVITY

In no way am I a psycho-analyst. I have wondered why I was such an insecure and timed child. I never felt at ease around anyone but our immediate family and that also included Aunt Matt's family. It was provoking for me to hear anyone and everyone who was a stranger say to me, "What's the matter? Cat's got your tongue?"

When I was two and a half or three years old, Mama permitted Sarah to take me to the well to see syrup making. Sarah darted about and I got lost. Smoke filled my eyes. A woman whom I did not recognize appeared. It was Aunt Sallie who had returned from another state to visit Aunt Matt. She took my hand and spoke kindly to me. She simply found Sarah and led us both home. She was the first and only stranger I felt at ease around. A few years later, Papa's cousin from California came to visit us. In a like friendly way she talked to me without ever asking a question. Some member of the family had remarked that she was a Christian Scientist. I had no idea what a Christian Scientist was but I immediately wanted to be one. That wish intensified when after returning to California, she sent me the first postcard that I had ever received.

On one occasion, a man whom I had never seen and to whom I had refused to talk with said, "They ought to put a prop under your head and make you hold up your head and make you talk". How I loathed him. I could visualize someone placing a jack like the one used to grease buggies under my chin.

When Blake and Sarah wished to go to some place and did not wish me to go along with them, they had two ways of dispelling me. They had previously told about having seen the stork deliver me with only a diaper on and had deposited me in the bed with Mama. Then the stork had said "Flip-Flop" and flew away. When they would say "Flip-Flop", I would return home crying. I think that it was the idea of someone seeing me clad in only my breech cloth that was embarrassing.

When Aunt Sallie died, her funeral was held up at Aunt Matt's house. We three children had attended. Shall We Gather at the River was sung. All that Sarah and Blake had to do to send me off in tears was to sing or hum a few bars of that song.

Sarah used to say, "Crook your finger at Beatrice and she will cry!" and I would.

DROUGHT AND DOWNPOUR

One morning when Papa made his semi-annual trip to Macon, Mama asked him to bring back a few cabbage plants. Instead of fifteen or twenty plants, Papa brought back three hundred. Mama was exasperated. It proved that this was a life-saving act. A garden was planted. It was so dry that nothing germinated. I think that we lived on dried black-eyed peas and cabbage that summer. Richard tried to be consoling by telling us that we must remember that each day without rain meant that we were one day closer to rain.

There came a time when the "ox was in a ditch." Willie had cut a field of grass for hay. It lay spreading out at the Sanders Place. On Sunday about noon, there was the sound of thunder. A large amount of cow feed was endangered. Papa felt that it would not violate the Sabbath to hitch up the wagon and to haul in the hay, because if the cattle did not get food during the winter they would die. We four girls went to help finish unloading it in the barn before the torrential downpour came thereby saving several weeks of food for the cows.

RIVER, CLODDY BOTTOM AND BUZZARDS

It was an enjoyable occasion when we could amble off to the river. Farther down the river is an approximate fifty foot wide and sixty feet or more of shore of flat rock. On it are several depressions which are said to have been worn out by the Indians grinding corn. It is also said that our great-grandparents could hear the pounding as they turned their corn into meal. From this level of rock there arises a very steep hill. It always seemed to me that it formed an 80 degree angle with the earth.

Somewhere near the top of this hill which precipitates from the fishery is a very cold spring of water. One wonders how such a cold spring could form at that altitude.

There was an area called the Cloddy Bottom. At one time, it had been cultivated. When it was plowed and the ground was too wet, clods of dirt formed. It was not cultivated since I can remember. Near the Cloddy Bottom were enormous rock projections protruding from the side. On or beneath these overhanging shelves of rocks the vultures nested and raised their young. We called these birds "buzzards". The eggs were laid on the bare ground with only a semblance of a nest. The eggs were almost twice the size of hens' eggs. The eggs are white with a few black spots on them. Baby buzzards are white. Of course, we never touched one of these filthy birds, but the birds are so helpful in disposing of animal carcasses.

Aunt Clyde told us of an interesting experience of her childhood. She and her sister found a vulture's nest in an old abandoned house. They saw the baby vultures and thought they were beautiful! They decided to take one home with them. A girl got on each side of the creature, each girl taking the tip of a wing. Swinging it between them they carried it home. Needless to say, their mother hurriedly sent them to return the little creature to its home.

PRANKS

Sometimes we played pranks on each other. I was outside playing. Allyne called me and told me that a hen had come from the blackberry vines, cackling. There must be a nest there. Finding a hen's nest was always exciting and fun. Within a few minutes, I had found the nest. There were a dozen or more eggs in it. I ran to the window telling Allyne to bring me a container to put the eggs in. She did. I returned to the nest and began to pick up the eggs. They were very, very light. I turned one over to find a hole in it. In fact, there was a hole in every one of them. Allyne yelled, "April fool!" I realized it was indeed April 1.

Richard and Milton delighted in playing pranks on Aunt Matt. One afternoon, Mama killed and dressed several chickens. Milton purloined one of the heads. He carried it to Aunt Matt's barn, climbed high up and implanted the chicken's head just beneath the roof of the barn. That afternoon when Aunt Matt went to milk the cow, Milton just "happened by" and engaged Aunt Matt in a casual conversation. After some minutes Milton said, "Aunt Matt, isn't that a chicken up there under the roof?" Aunt Matt was sorely baffled. She was puzzled and conjectured about how it could have happened. After having his fun, Milton confessed.

After he started working for the railroad, on his trips home, Milton usually brought home a gift for both Mama and Aunt Matt. On one weekend visit, Milton brought Aunt Matt a box of chocolate covered cherries. She thanked him profusely. At that moment, he dropped a little rubber snake into her lap. She yelled loudly enough to be heard a half a mile away.

"Here, take your old candy and go home!" she yelled. He had not intended to frighten her so badly. He apologized and peace reigned.

Several years later, Richard donned a mustache, a false nose, some over-sized spectacles and some shabby trousers. Aunt Matt did not see him until he tapped on the wall by the doorstep. She emitted one of the most blood-curdling yells. Sarah, who had gone ahead to witness the scene, said, "What is it, Aunt Matt?"

"It's the devil, I think!" shouted Aunt Matt. Richard turned to go around the house. Aunt Matt recognized him.

CHICKENS

As a small child, a most disgusting sight to me was that of a picture of a beautiful fluffy baby chick standing erect and flapping its little wings while standing by an empty eggshell. I knew at that time that eggs were incubated for twenty-one days. When the hatching day came, the chick on the inside began pecking on the egg shell. We then said, "The egg has popped." It required an hour or more for the shell to be open wide enough for the chick to emerge. Even when it did, it was a helpless, weak and wet little fellow. It needed the exercise of pecking the shell to strengthen it. It required an entire day for a nest full of biddies to hatch, dry out, and walk around.

After they were ready to leave the nest, they were placed in an old newspaper-lined bucket to be transferred to a coop which had previously been prepared for them. A cloth covered them to keep them from becoming chilled during their trip to their first home. One of us children often carried the chicks while the other toted the mother hen. She had lost weight from brooding. She was fed well and watered.
The chicks were several days old before the mother hen and her brood were allowed to go out of the coop and forage under the bushes and in the grass. When the first peal of thunder sounded, Mama went out and called the hen who led her biddies directly to the coop.

Aunt Matt had a brood that didn't quite make it home. They were not babies but had developed some feathers. As we viewed the helpless chicks, Aunt Matt detected some sign of life. She hastily picked them up, put them into her lap and carried them to her kitchen. She built a small fire in her kitchen stove, lined the oven with newspaper and placed the unconscious chicks in the oven. She left the door to the oven open so that she could tend to the recuperating chicks. Every one of them recovered.

Sarah had a flock of sixteen chickens that was not as fortunate. She was beginning to train them to go into the chicken house to roost. I didn't understand what she was trying to do. I saw them all piled into one coop. One was sitting in the doorway. I pushed him with my foot and closed the coop. The next morning there were sixteen dead fryers, all smothered.

Baby chicks are covered with a soft down. When they are several weeks or a month old they lose this down and grow feathers. Sometimes a chick loses his down before the feathers are present to replace the down. We had one unfortunate chick that had lost all of his feathers. He was stark naked. Other chicks his age pecked him. Mildred and I adopted him. We found a box to house him. He had a hearty appetite. One night we placed a bountiful supply of corn before him. He ate. And he ate. His crop became full and yet the greedy little fellow continued to eat. We saw the impression of corn in his neck. He ate until his little throat was filled to the back of his mouth. He began to gasp for breath. Mildred began to panic. Neither of us wanted to see our little pet die. I picked him up by his little feet, turned him upside down and gave him a few shakes. After regurgitating a dozen grains of corn, he seemed to be relieved. I placed him back on his feet. He lived happily after that.

When a chick died during his first few weeks of life, it was my duty to inter him. I crammed a deceased chicken into a matchbox. After some time, I wished to dis-inter him and see if the feathers, flesh and bones had decomposed when to my horror, a swarm of flies flew out. I ran. I did not know what was left.

During the hot summer months, I often slept on a pallet on the porch upstairs. One night, I was awakened by the squawking of a chicken. My first thought was that either a weasel or an opossum was trying to get a dainty morsel for his midnight snack. Clad in my pajamas, I jumped up and ran downstairs and out of the front door. I saw nothing and I heard nothing. The next morning I told Allyne about my experience. She strongly reprimanded me for doing such a dangerous thing. She told me that it could have been a two-legged thief. Never again did I go out of the house at night alone.

TIN ROOF

One stormy night we were just finishing supper when Willie came rushing in. (He had been late completing some task in the field.) He hastened upstairs to confirm that all of his windows were fastened securely. When he came back through the dining room, he headed for the kitchen to wash his hands. He said, "The tin is flying!"

I let out a yell thinking that a 6 x 10 ft. section of the roof was blowing away and water would soon be flooding the house. Hearing my despairing cry, Papa asked, "What is it?"

"The roof is flying!" I replied.

"Where?" he asked.

"In the attic." I explained. He leaped from the table and hastened to the hall, grabbed the lamp that was kept lit at night until bedtime. Up the stairs he went looking like the Statue of Liberty as he ascended the steps. When he reached the landing between the stairs and attic, he paused looking out the window toward the chicken coop. With a bewildered expression, he asked, "What in the world is Miss (his pet name for Mama) doing at the hen house?"

I tried to clarify myself by explaining that the tin roof on our attic was blowing off. He snorted in disgust, letting me know that there was no tin on our attic roof. It was my time to be surprised. We never reached the attic. Willie was only informing us that the tin was blowing off a nearby chicken coop.

TOM, DICK, AND HARRY

An article appeared in some magazine about teenagers overcoming timidity. I wondered if I could apply it. On the first Sunday in August each year, the Sardis Congregational Church held an all day singing with dinner on the grounds. We attended. I thought that the singing was sublime. As we spread our dinner with the others I saw an attractive boy whom I had never seen before. He was with two other boys whom I knew but did not much admire. I would forego their presence to meet the "cute" boy. I learned that he was their cousin.

Sarah and I conversed with them until time to go back into the church. Here is when I decided to use my newly found advice on how to overcome timidity and feel at ease around boys. I actually invited them up to visit. Twelve year old Mildred and her friend, Harriet, were lurking in the background with their ears attuned to our conversation.

When we reached home we did our chores but were not hungry when Papa and Mama ate. Later we four girls nibbled on sandwiches and left-over desserts. The next day Mildred and Harriet slept late. At lunch time they were in high gear with hilarity and verbosity. The day was a scorcher! Mama had rather reluctantly agreed that we could go to the creek. The water was hardly deep enough to swim in but we could cool off. As we sat around the table talking, Mildred and Harriet did what I feared. They began to tell about

Tom, Dick and Harry. They even told about me asking them to come up to visit. Mama looked a little disgusted but Papa chuckled about it.

Outside, the hungry dogs began to bark. Papa laughingly remarked that perhaps it was my friends, the Jackson boys. I doubted it but I volunteered to go to the door to see what had set the dogs afire with barking. There were the two brothers, each dressed in a dark blue serge suit complete with ties and coats. Perspiration was dripping...No. Sweat was pouring down the side of their faces onto their clothing. I invited them to be seated in the swing which was the coolest available spot. It seems Harry had had to return home to the little hamlet of Dry Branch. Tom and Dick had hitched a ride on a lumber truck to the mailbox and had walked the short distance to the house.

All of the family came out to greet the guest. I don't know who washed the dishes. I didn't. That was the only redeeming feature of the day. One by one some of the family members left to do their duties or interests that lay in the house, but not Mildred and Harriet. They wanted to see all, hear all, and know all.

Mildred had converted Papa to the fact that **Old Maid** did not make one infamous. I suggested to the boys that we could play **Set Back, Rook,** or even **Old Maid**. They graciously thanked us but said that they did not play cards. Next, I suggested that we play **Pollyanna or Parcheesi**. When they learned that dice was involved in the game, they rejected that also.

I felt that the boys thought that we girls were trying to lure them to Hell. Sarah for once was quiet. I think that she secretly pitied me. We had neither Tiddly Winks nor Dominoes to offer. The day had been a disaster for me. Mildred and Harriet had found it most entertaining and no regrets about foregoing the trip to the creek.

AWAY FROM HOME

We seldom spent the night away from home. I did go with Ruby Gresham once when I was in the fourth or fifth grade. The family radiated with love for one another. Bible readings and prayer were held before retiring and before breakfast in the morning. I slept that night between Nellie and Ruby, all of us in our union suits.

I do not remember clearly about my first night in the city. Uncle Dick Burden and Aunt Minnie invited me. I presume that they came for me. They lived at the corner of Vineville Avenue and Hines Terrace. I went for a walk alone around the block. At night I was served a new dish, gelatin. I did not like it but I politely ate every spoonful of it. That night when I was ushered upstairs to retire, Aunt Minnie turned on the water for my bath. She left me on my own. There I stood watching the water flow into the tub. I just didn't know how much water to allow to flow in. In the first place, I had never been in a bath tub before and I didn't want to be extravagant. I had heard that city people had to pay for water. After three inches of water had flowed in, I climbed in.

One summer Cousin Nola Jackson and her three children came by on their way home from services at Caney Creek Primitive Baptist Church. I was invited to accompany them home and stay a week. I was overjoyed. I had never stayed more than one night away from home at a time. I had a delightful visit. Near the end of the week, I began experiencing nostalgia. Edna and Reba said that they would teach me to read and write Latin and Greek. I agreed. Edna went running into the house. Reba and I squatted down. Each of us had a little six inch long stick. As Reba incanted "Pour down upon me", we made marks on the ground. On the "Pour down upon me", Edna poured a glass of water upon me. I cried. Cousin Nola lightly punished Edna. I was so ashamed of myself. The water did not hurt me. I was just plain homesick. When Willie came to get me, I was relieved.

SARA MARVIN

Just when I became a friend of Sara Marvin Barron, I do not remember. We didn't start to school at the same time. She had probably lived in Macon. We called her mother "Miss Oscie". She came to keep house for her widowed father, Mr. Sam Hodge. They lived down by the river in a little yellow house. It was located near what is now the end of the Sam Hodge Bridge over the river in Jones County. Her mother always welcomed me with love and friendliness. It was relaxing to go to sleep listening to the lulling river. Too, they always served fish.

Always, I had rough ugly hands. Miss Oscie noticed them. She suggested that I get cow urine to bathe my hands. I was horrified. I could never do that.

Mama gave me permission to spend the night with Sara Marvin. When I returned home, I told Mama that we visited a neighbor of theirs and one of the children had the measles. Mama exploded with anxiety. It was as if I had walked into a case of bubonic plague.

Often Sara Marvin and her sister, Edna, went to their Aunt Jessie's house for lunch during the big recess hour. She invited me to go with her one day. At first, I refused because I knew that Jessie had not invited me. Sara Marvin insisted. I went. I shall never forget Jessie's haggard look when she saw Sara Marvin dragging me in for lunch. No doubt she had worked hard that morning. She had a small child and was over-burdened with work. I did not know what to do. I sat down at the table. I believe that all that she had was string beans and cornbread. I served myself. When I tasted the beans, I found that they were the saltiest beans that had ever entered my mouth. Since I was an uninvited guest and, I believe, an unwanted guest, I was conscience stricken and did not know anything to do but eat them. Never again was I invited to have lunch at Jessie's house. I can guess why.

One summer when I was thirteen years old, I spent a week with Sara Marvin. A vacation Bible School was being held at the Wayside Presbyterian Church. Transportation was furnished. We went. The morning was divided into sections of classes: Bible Study, Art, Recreation and Needlework. Sara Marvin doted on the needlework. I was intrigued with Bible Study. I had never heard of the Apostle Paul and his missionary journeys. Reverend Manning taught the class and he made it so very interesting. I eagerly anticipated the next episode each day.

In the afternoon we went down to Mr. Hodge's mill and waded out into the shoals where the water was knee deep. I wore one of Sara Marvin's swim suits. If Mama had known that I was dabbling around in the river, she would have had Willie hitch up the buggy and fetch me home.

One afternoon, Sara Marvin went up the hill to do her chore, milk the cow. She went to the cowpen and she placed the milk bucket on a shelf. The grass on the outside of the cowpen looked so green and inviting! She decided to roll down the slope. In so doing, she rolled over a freshly deposited pile of dung. She was smeared from chest down in the mess. Both the front and the back of her dress were covered with the feces. She quickly jumped up and quickly headed back down the hill toward home. I followed a safe distance behind her wondering how she would get into the house without contaminating the entire house. When she reached the house, she did not turn in at the short driveway. She proceeded fifty yards beyond the house and plunged into the river. Being a good swimmer, she swam until she was acceptably clean. She emerged from the water, entered the house, took a bath, donned clean clothes and milked the cow.

THE PARKS

Laura was like one of us. Hers was a large family. Our family members paired off well together. Charlie claimed Frances as his girl while John Henry claimed Sarah. Neither Laurie nor I were interested in boys. Being the same age we played together. The same was true of Louise and Mildred. On Saturday afternoons and Sundays we all got together and had as much fun as any young folks could have.

One Sunday afternoon we all boarded an empty flat-bed lumber truck and went riding up toward Juliette. As we rode along, a sudden rain cloud engulfed us and poured down. Ida Belle, who was rather sickly, was with us. We all knew that we would "catch thunder" if it leaked out that she had gotten wet. We saw a deserted house glimmering through the woods. We all got out, found enough dry leaves and limbs to kindle a hot roaring fire. Soon everybody was thoroughly dry and we resumed our riding.

On our return trip home we came upon a carload of strangers. Their car was stalled. They needed help to push it off to get it started. We were quite willing to give our assistance but inquired why one youth was sitting on the back seat and not helping. The reply was, "He's holding the battery water." We knew he was holding illicit moonshine and was under the influence of the said drug.

After a year of wonderful evenings and holidays our Parks friends moved to Guntersville, Alabama. Although correspondence ensued, we've never seen them since.

NEW HOPE

Our very limited social life was centered around the New Hope Primitive Baptist Church, of which Papa was a member. Meetings were held on the fourth Saturday and the fourth Sunday of each month. I have been told that the Saturday service was to commemorate the Sabbath and the Sunday service was to observe the Lord's Day. Papa never referred to his house of worship as a church but he always said "meeting house".

Mama would allow one or two of us to go each time. She seldom attended. Instrumental music was forbidden. I can remember the lovely songs being acapella. After a thirty minute song service there followed an equally long prayer service. That was followed by an hour and a half sermon. If another preacher were present, the sermon might last even longer. The sermons were delivered in a thunderous sing song tone.

Baptism was by total immersion. Aunt Matt told of Milton's witnessing his first baptism. Aunt Matt asked him, "What did the preacher say when he baptized the man?" "Go to swimming, my brother", was Milton's reply.

The preacher best liked by us children was Elder Ben Williamson from Lizella. Charlie reasoned since Papa called him "Brother", then he must be our Uncle. We affectionately called him by that name, which he apparently enjoyed. He was a chubby jovial man.

Each year an associational meeting was held. Ten or more churches composed an association. It was seldom that it was held at New Hope. Unimproved roads made it necessary for the members who had to travel many miles to spend a couple of nights at the host church. There were twenty-two visitors to be our guest one night. We youngsters slept on pallets while the guests occupied the beds. Some of the male visitors slept on the floor.

Aunt Matt agreed to have a couple of guests to stay in her guest room. At nine or ten o'clock, Aunt Matt went down to claim her guests. She was tired after helping Mama to prepare the meals and sleeping accommodations. When Aunt Matt approached her prospective guests, one of the women said, "I am singing now!"

Aunt Matt, being a great mimic, related that to us in a falsetto voice. Aunt Matt was disgusted but waited patiently while a few more songs were song. After assigning the two guests to their room, Aunt Matt was ready to turn in herself. The women hurriedly undressed and hurriedly donned their nighties. They climbed into the bed and one of them let out a shriek, "You've got clean sheets on the bed. I've got to get up and wash my feet." When Aunt Matt related this to us, we howled with laughter. Just what did the woman expect?

HOLY SPIRIT

Most people, in giving testimony of receiving the gift of the Holy Spirit have experienced some interesting and startling event. I have not. Since we did not have a radio, I had not heard any great evangelist causing a great reformation. And I cannot remember anyone talking to me about my soul or my relationship to God. When I was ten or twelve years old, I read one of Willie's books entitled **First Steps for Little Feet**. I became aware of Jesus Christ and what He had done for me. There was a yearning for someone to whom I could discuss my feelings. There was nobody. Most people can tell you the day, hour and the place when they first believed. I cannot.

Even today, there are so very few people with whom I can express my innermost thoughts. I think that I was about sixteen years old that I made my first public profession of faith. No minister ever questioned me or discussed my feelings about the Lord. When I walked down the aisle, the only question asked me was "Do you take Jesus Christ as your personal Savior and Lord?" I was baptized in the Ocmulgee River, a few yards north of the Hodge Bridge.

FOLLOW-UP BROTHERS

During these days, Richard became a sawyer and stayed most of the time at home. Both Milton and Charlie became firemen for the Southern Railway. Since Willie had had respiratory problems during his stay in the Army, Papa insisted that he stay at home in the open air and become a farmer. Willie did not want to be a farmer but since he did not have the financial resources to attend college and become a civil engineer, he did stay home. He read profusely and remembered everything that he read. He became a learned historian and could talk on almost any subject that one could broach.

Hiram enlisted in the Army. He had wanted to do so earlier but was too young. Now he enlisted. One term was enough for him. He next went to Florida where he worked in the orange industry. Next he went to the Mid-West where he worked in the wheat fields. He worked on a barge on the Mississippi River. During the Depression years, he worked at any job he could find, however menial it could be. He told of once working in a tannery. The odor there was terrific but it was the only job available. He saved enough money to attend a movie. When he entered the movie house and was seated, people moved away from him. He then realized it was because of the stench of his only shoes. Many years later when I visited him, he drove me to the sand dunes along a lake and showed me where he and another vagrant shared a can of pork and beans. The beans were heated in the can over a small fire.

Finally, he secured a job in the automobile industry where he remained until his retirement. During those years while employed in the auto industry, when the plant closed down for inventory each year, he traveled. He visited every state in the Union. He visited every industry that he encountered. He even obtained permission to enter a coal mine. He was widely educated in every industry one could imagine.

One year when he was at home, he bought an Edison phonograph and thirty or more records. It was the first music to which we were exposed.

A year or so later, Hiram invited us four girls to accompany him on a trip to Florida. The only stipulation was that we must travel light. Allyne went to town and purchased for each of us a pair of white pants. This and with changes of underwear we set out. We left early and ate breakfast with Grandpa and Grandma. From there, we headed to Silver Springs, Florida. We spent the night there after riding over Silver Springs in a glass bottom boat ride down the river. The next night we spent at Fort Myers. At that time, Ft Myers was a relatively small town. It had myriads of mosquitoes. The next day we went through the Everglades on the Tamiami Trail. I was most impressed with the Indian Village that we visited. We enjoyed the cool morning air. Hiram stopped by the side of the canal, dipped up some water and shaved. The next night we were in St Augustine. There we toured the city and of course visited the prison then called Fort Marion. Somewhere along the coast, Hiram decided to take us on a ride on the beach. We sped along but when we slowed, the wheels sank into the sand. Hiram saw that the situation was hopeless. The tide was coming in. He instructed us to remove the luggage if the water reached the car. With that, he crossed over to the highway and was hurrying to a nearby town. Soon after he left, a carload of men riding on the highway saw our dilemma and alighted from their car and came over. They lifted Hiram's car from the sand. We all chipped in. Sarah cranked the car and away we traveled, overtaking Hiram still trotting toward town for help. Was he relieved when we stopped beside him! After spending the night there, we headed back to Macon. It was a rather uneventful day. As we whizzed along, we encountered a young goat with its head caught in the fence. Hiram stopped the car and got out and released him.

SHERMAN

The story of Sherman's march through Georgia has been told and re-told to every Jarrell generation. I shall recount it as it was told to me. Grandpa Jarrell was too old to serve in the Confederate Army. He was given the responsibility of advising and supervising the farms left behind.

When it was learned that Sherman's army was headed toward the Jarrell farm, Grandpa instructed a freed slave to dig a hole under the cane mashes, place the cured meat in the hole and re-cover it with the cane mashes. The man did as told.

Later when the Army came, the ex-slave was asked the whereabouts of the meat. The ex-slave told. The soldiers dug but not deep enough. Thinking that he had lied they strung him up over the barn door. After the soldiers left, the ex-slave was rescued but was in an unconscious state.

1847 House

Aunt Matt's House

AUNT MATT AND FAMILY

Before launching into the introduction of Aunt Matt's family, I must tell you a bit about her early background. As a little girl she went to stay with her half-sister to attend school. Her teacher was Mr. Dykes, a stern disciplinarian. I do not know what minor infraction of the rules she committed but he inflicted a most severe beating. Aunt Ellen told Aunt Matt's father about it. He went to see Mr. Dykes and asked him not to be so severe on such a little girl. He assented to Grandpa's request. Soon after Grandpa left, Mr. Dykes inflicted a more severe beating for tattling. That ended Aunt Matt's schooling.

Aunt Matt and Grandma Jarrell took four of Grandma's grandchildren to rear. Uncle Bob had died of typhoid fever. His wife, Aunt Lula was physically, financially and emotionally unable to rear the four children. I shall give as brief account of each of them as I remember them.

Randolph, we called him Randy, did a lot of laughing and talking. He left home for the United States Army. He returned when the war was over and became a conductor on the Central Georgia Railroad.

Ida Belle, unfortunately was an epileptic. In those days, families tried to keep such a malady from the public eye, as if it were a disgrace. There was little medication. Aunt Matt, I presume, had taught her to read and she read beautifully. She was a sweet and obliging girl. She was my favorite of the four siblings. She would read to us and tell us stories. In today's society, she would be an asset to a nursery school.

Annie had a vivacious personality. She was ten years older than I. I always admired Annie.

Ed was an awkward teenager. As he arose from the table he inadvertently stepped in the churn filled with clabber. We all thought it was funny. Aunt Matt didn't see anything funny about it at all.

The house in which Aunt Matt lived was on a hill that was about 100 yards from our home.

Aunt Matt inherited this family home where she cared for Grandma Jarrell until her death. The house had an upstairs. We children were warned not to go upstairs. We were told that there lived Raw Head and Bloody Bones.

Aunt Matt had read and educated herself until she was in her teens. She traveled to Atlanta and enrolled in a business school. She boarded in a house that housed several other girls. Each morning, the host held a devotional meeting at which the Bible was read and prayer was offered. It was an unduly long supplication.

Blessings were evoked for everyone from the lowest servant to the President of the United States. One morning he surprised the girls by asking one of them to pray. It happened to be Aunt Matt. As everybody bowed their heads, Aunt Matt was so taken aback that she blurted out, "God, bless the President of the United States". She jumped up and fled to her room upstairs.

For her existence, Aunt Matt operated a little store. It was held in the room adjoining the dining room. She sold various imperishable commodities such as snuff, tobacco, lard, coffee and candy.

Aunt Matt had a number of interesting books which she shared with any of us who wished to read them. I think that she had all of Gene Stratton Porter's books which revealed many facts about nature accompanied by a love story. Aunt Matt could also tell stories most graphically with her fluent vocabulary. I can still remember how she enthralled us in telling the story of Joseph being sold into slavery down in Egypt. I can remember how she brought tears into my eyes as she read The Dog of Flanders.

One day Sarah, Blake and our cousin, Ruth Green, and I were sitting on the porch of the gin house. Our conversation turned to foods. We all agreed that food away from home often tasted better than that at home. We talked about how good Aunt Matt's biscuits tasted. Ruth announced that she had spent the night at Aunt Matt's and that she had had a plate of biscuits left over from breakfast. They, the other three, decided that we must go up there and get them. I did not want to participate in this theft but I lacked the fortitude to voice my conviction. We went on up to Aunt Matt's house and tip-toed into the hall. Aunt Matt was on the porch sweeping. We saw neither Annie nor Ida. I dutifully held out the lap of my apron while the plate of biscuits were poured into it. We tip-toed out of the hall and went behind her garden to eat them. How the other three smacked and enjoyed the biscuits. I could hardly enjoy the first one because of the guilt that choked me. I resolved never to participate in theft again.

Years later, I worked in a peach cannery during the summer. I worked on the night shift. As I worked the early hours of the night, I saved some of the juiciest peaches for my midnight snack dessert. It was years after that when I realized that I had been involved in stealing again. I have asked God to forgive me for the four or five cans of peaches I ate that summer.

SCHOOL

The biggest surprise that I experienced in my early childhood was the day Mama said that I could go to school. She dressed me in a white middy blouse and a multi-colored striped skirt. Of course the skirt was attached to the bodice. I had never seen the outfit before. I still have no idea where the clothes came from.

I remember nothing of the trip to school but I do remember my arrival. Two big girls came out to meet us. They were the Mitchell sisters. Being among the oldest girls there, they took me under their wing. They wore identical striped dresses with skirts fastened to a bodice high above the waist line, forming a ruffle.

The little one-room school house had two doors that opened onto a porch. There were three windows on each side of the room. Between the windows was a dark fabric looking like oilcloth. It was called a blackboard. There were two rows of double desks in the room. Near the back were large double desks and toward the front were smaller double desks.

At the other end of the room was a raised area. Some called it a platform. Others called it a stage. On one side of the platform was a beat-up organ that could still emit a few squeaks and a recognizable tune. On the other side was a sand table. The sand table had a three inch high fence around its top. Within was a thin layer of sand. A piece of glass simulated a pond on which were two or three celluloid ducks. Miniature plants simulating trees were scattered about on the sand table.

On the walls were posted six or eight pictures about twelve by twenty-four inches. I don't know how or when I had learned to read but the picture had written on it:

Higgly, Piggly, my black hen.
She lays eggs for a gentleman.
The gentleman comes each day
To see what my black hen doth lay.

Two more objects were introduced to me, a pencil sharpener and a trash basket. I realized that the pencil sharpener was a vast improvement over the knives used at home to sharpen pencils. After hearing the word "trash basket", I thought that when the student body was saying the model prayer in the morning they were saying "….and forgive us for our trashbaskets as we forgive those who trashbasket us."

On the porch between the two doors was a shelf on which a five gallon water cooler set. Each morning two boys went up the hill to get water from Mrs. Ida Mitchell's well. Each of us children was required to bring a drinking cup to be kept in a designated spot. Frank Glover, my cousin, carried his collapsible drinking cup in his back pocket. Even when we played "Hiding" we could always know where Frank was by the rattle of the cup in his hip pocket.

Seemingly, Miss Irene, the teacher, did not call upon me to read the first day. However, when that fateful day arrived that she did call upon me, I balked. I had never said a word to that woman and I had no intentions of ever saying a word to her. To read and let the multitude hear me was unthinkable! The multitude consisted of sixteen or eighteen students. Miss Irene brought her chair down from her desk upon the stage and set it down by my little desk. She ordered me to read. I knew every word in that unattractive and unappealing little primer but I was not about to utter a word. Miss Irene produced a switch, and began to nettle my legs. I began, "I (sniff, sniff) have a (sniff, sniff) flag. (sniff, sniff) The flag I have. (sniff, sniff) Is it not (sniff, sniff) a pretty flag?" I did not see anything pretty about the flag.

In the entire book, there were only two pretty pages. On page three, there was a picture of a pretty girl who faintly looked like Bessie. On another page was a blondish boy playing with his rabbits. "Our Bennie Boy has a pretty little rabbit. Our Bennie Boy has two pretty rabbits" and so on until Our Bennie Boy had ten pretty little rabbits. By now, I presume that Our Bennie Boy has ten million pretty little rabbits.

To call our school to order at the beginning of the day or after recess, it was customary that the teacher ring a bell. We called this "taking in". How the students vied for the privilege of "taking in"…All, except me. I wanted no part of it. Finally, on a fated day as recess was ending, Miss Irene said, "Beatrice, go ring the bell."

I refused. I just could not bring myself to stand before that enormous body of sixteen students and ring that bell. Miss Irene was a determined lady…just a little more determined than I was, or shall I say, "stronger" than I was. She took me by the arm and pulled or dragged me to the little school building, up the steps and to the teacher's desk. She picked up the bell, placed it into my hand, closed my fingers over the handle of the bell, and pulled me out onto the porch. There before that enormous throng of perhaps sixteen children she raised and lowered my arm to cause the bell to ring. I cried a full gallon of tears and was more embarrassed than I would be today to do a strip tease before sixteen thousand people.

Winters were cold but we had a two-eye heater which was anchored in a box of sand. As we entered the room in cold weather, we were allowed to go near the heater to warm ourselves provided we were mousey quiet.

Parents provided the wood for the fire to heat the school room. I can only remember three parents who brought wood for our school. They were Papa, Uncle Tom Glover and Mr. Wilke Gresham. I assume that they were the only parents who had a wagon and access to wood.

Fifty or more yards back of the schoolhouse was the girls' privy, a four-holer. I soon observed that when various girls raised their hands and went up and whispered something to the teacher, the teacher would nod her head and the girl hurried out of the room and rushed to the privy. It did not take a simpleton to figure it out. When I became brave enough and felt desperate enough, I raised my hand and marched up to the teacher and whispered, "May I go out to pee?"

Later, I learned inadvertently that I was supposed to say, "May I be excused?"

Another embarrassment…Another gallon of tears.

We all awaited "big recess". Lunch time. When I think of lunches, I still think of the little blue enamel bucket in which we carried our lunches. For lunch, our typical fare was scrambled eggs in a biscuit, jam or jelly in a biscuit, sometimes a slice of ham in a biscuit and always a sweet potato. Some of the boys brought their lunch to school in a gallon lard bucket. I don't know what all was in the bucket but they would often have a small bottle of syrup which they poured into the lid of the bucket and then sopped the syrup with a plain biscuit.

The remainder of the noon recess period was in playing games. One game played was called Hail Over. It was a rather senseless game but everyone seemingly enjoyed it. One person was "It". "It" stayed on one side of the building while the others went to the opposing side of the building. "It" threw the ball over at the same time yelling "Hail Over". If the ball were caught, all ran toward "It's" side, trying to avoid being caught. After playing Hail Over for a few weeks, we played other games. One game was called Poison. We drew a circle, varying in size according to the number of participants. We held hands and endeavored to pull someone into the circle. That person was then Poison. We dropped hands and ran to touch wood. Poison stood at a distance and counted to ten. The players had to run to another source of poison (wood) without being caught. If caught, that player was poisoned and had to join the catcher/chaser.

Another game was Stealing Sticks. Each side had a circle with twelve sticks in it. Each side tried to steal sticks from the opposing side. One day, Vernie was choosing. She said, "I'll take Beatrice. She's a game little chick." I had no idea what a game little chick happened to be about but I knew it was a compliment.

Fox and Geese was another game. Usually a large student was the "Fox". He stood in the middle of the road. The "Geese", the other students, stood on the side. When Fox said, "Geese, all pass over", they crossed. The Fox tried to catch someone who would struggle to get away. If unsuccessful within 30 seconds, that goose became a fox also and the game continued until all were caught.

There was an expression "King's Excuse". That was said when one wanted to explain something about the game. He was exempt from getting caught while the explanation was made.

A young student misunderstood "King's Excuse" and said, "Skin the goose". From then on we all said, "Skin the goose".

In playing games at school, I was never frightened except on one occasion. We were playing a game in which I was being chased. A big boy was chasing me. He had a leering expression and gait like Mama's old "Dominecker" rooster trying to copulate with hen. He even had one foot raised, I imagined. I hastily eluded him and always tried to stay out of his pathway. I never told anyone.

ANOTHER SCHOOL YEAR

It was school opening time again. Miss Irene had married and moved to California. Allyne went to Grandpa's house to live and attend high school.

Miss Carrie was our new teacher. Annie Florence was the chauffer of the buggy that year. Although I disliked Miss Irene, all of the big girls liked her very much. Annie Florence, being one of the big girls, formed a distaste for Miss Carrie. Winter time came. Miss Carrie required us to stay in our seats away from the stove. The little heater was turned so that the warmest part was toward the teacher's desk. Annie grew aggravated with her. One day Annie Florence urged the old horse just a little faster than usual. We reached school much earlier than usual. Annie knew the way to get in by way of the locked window. She climbed in, unlocked the door and bade us to enter. We turned the stove around so that the students could benefit most by the heat. Fire was built in the heater. It was hot when Miss Carrie arrived but Miss Carrie was even hotter. That afternoon when the fire had cooled down, Miss Carrie had the able-bodied boys turn the stove back. The heating problem was still unsolved.

That was the year that a new steel bridge was built over Falling Creek. With construction work and grading going on, a temporary crossing was made so that Annie could drive safely across the creek. We children had to walk across on boards on the old bridge. A series of rainy days came. The creek rose though not alarmingly. The authorities deemed that it was safe for Annie to drive across. As she drove, she looked like a queen with a regal air. How I envied her when she reached mid-stream and at the deepest part of the creek, the water rose on to the floor of the buggy. Annie frantically began grabbing books, lunches and a few wraps. She was able to save everything.

On some days, we walked to school. As we walked, we were feeling exhilarated. At one place we reached an exceedingly high bank on the roadside. We were challenged to see who could go highest on the bank. I am sure that I was not the winner. The next day Papa had business down the road. His hawk-eyes never missed a thing. Needless to say, we received a lecture about scouring up the bank like a herd of goats.

I really enjoyed my reading program under Miss Carrie. The poems of Robert Louis Stevenson, the story of the life of Rosa Bonheur and the history stories of George Washington were a few of my favorites.

For the next few years my teacher was Miss Jewel. She had recently graduated from G.N. I., Georgia Normal Institute. The name later changed to Georgia State College for Women, better known as G.S.C.W. Later it was called Georgia College State and University.

Miss Jewel boarded with Mrs. Sallie Green. Miss Jewel had a boyfriend whose name was Elmer. Each afternoon she assigned us "busy work" while she wrote to Elmer. If my work involved geography, I would find the smallest and the most remote town possible. I would then go up and tell her that I could not find it. While she feverishly tried to locate it, I would look over her shoulder and read her letter to Elmer. The salutations varied. On some days it was "Elmer, My Darling" and on others, it was "My Dearest Elmer". Unknowingly, she gave me a course in writing love letters.

My favorite subject that year was geography. The hardest lesson in the book was the one of geographical formations. I could easily understand rivers, lakes and peninsulas but I could not and to this day am not able to differentiate between a bay, gulf, sound, sea and a cape.

The basic fundamentals of whole numbers had never been difficult for me. Adding simple fractions had not been difficult but when it came to adding mixed fractions, I was lost. That night, at home, Mama taught me. She wrote the fractions down in a horizontal line. I could manipulate them very well. The next day the teacher said that the fractions would have to be placed in a vertical position. She finally got it through my thick skull how she wanted it done. My punishment was to stay in at recess and compose fifty examples on the board. This time I produced two gallons of tears. This staying in at recess time deprived me of play period. I don't know whether it deprived me of my lunch.

There was an unexplainable principle of education that was practiced by some when I was a child. "If you can't get it in to his head, get it in through his back with a stick." Poor George was a slow learner. I felt sorry for him. Sometimes a teacher was so unmerciful.

When I was in the fifth grade, Liberty School had the greatest enrollment that it ever had. Perhaps it was 30 or more students. A small village of four or five houses and commissary were built about a mile south of Falling Creek. Among the new fifth grade students were Mildred, Myrtice and Laura. Mildred had formally lived in Macon. Her father was a superintendent of some sawmilling area. She wore clothes of the latest style. Black sateen bloomers were in vogue that year. Dresses were worn just a little shorter than bloomers.

We liked Mildred and played happily with her at school. She was one whom we did not invite to our home nor did she invite us to hers. I wonder if this were the first time that I became aware of social class.

Myrtice was from a large family of workers for the sawmill. For some reason, neither did we visit her or were visited.

OTHER SCHOOL EVENTS

FIRST CHRISTMAS TREE

The year that I began school I saw my first Christmas tree. We had a Christmas program that year. The only thing I remember about the Christmas program that was presented, was that I was among a group of children who formed an acrostic with the words "MERRY CHRISTMAS". I held up my cardboard "S" and said, "Santa is jolly. He brought me a Dolly."

The tree was spectacular. I know that my mouth must have dropped open in amazement. We had exchanged names or names had been exchanged for us. I remember neither whose name I had drawn nor what I gave her. All presents exchanged were very inexpensive. Bessie's gift to her friend, Nellie, was a cake of store-bought soap. Mama had a new handkerchief for Sarah to give to her friend. Ruby had for me a small drinking glass covered with a blue jacket which her mother made from scraps of cloth. I thought it was beautiful and treasured it for many years.

The rural community in which we lived was an impoverished one. We all were poor and didn't know it. We and all our friends hung up a stocking at Christmas time and all of us received practically the same thing, an apple, an orange, a stick of candy, and a very, very inexpensive toy.

WORLD WAR I

During the year that the United States entered World War I, I saw my first airplane. Many people called them airships. Miss Irene dashed into the school house, grabbed the flag, ran out, and waved it. The pilot lowered a wing in acknowledgement of it.

Miss Irene also planned and planted a Victory Garden. I don't know what she planted in it. I only remember digging in it. She also staged a play on the out-door platform. It was entitled Mrs. Tubbs Does Her Bit. It depicted a patriotic woman essaying efforts showing patriotism. I had a part…one line. I found a hysterical woman's teeth under the table. To say my one line, one word "Teeth!" was no problem for me. I knew that was only play acting.

ALLYNE'S TEACHING

After graduating from high school Allyne attended college for one summer session. She was able to obtain a provisional license. She became my seventh grade teacher. And a very efficient one she was! She vied only with Mrs. Hattie Chiles at Gray.

When Allyne became an instructor, Papa insisted that we drive a mule to school because there was not a horse available. We all really had rather walked than ride behind an unpredictable old mule. We never argued with Papa so we had no voice in the matter. Cars were few and far between. Whenever a motor vehicle was heard, we got out of the buggy and someone went up to the mule's head and held her bridle until the vehicle had passed.

When we reached the school, the mule was unhitched. Before removing her bridle a rope was tied around her neck. She was then anchored to a tree. One day, whoever was responsible for tying the rope goofed. A slip knot was tied. Soon the rope was pulled tight and the mule began to choke. Allyne grabbed a knife which was kept and stowed in her desk drawer. She used it to cut the rope and free the choking mule. It also freed her to run. With my pessimistic personality, instantly I could imagine all kinds of catastrophes such as us marooned three miles from home with an empty buggy and a set of harness including a bridle, while a crazy mule probably was wondering as far as Jasper County and Papa as angry as a hornet. Fortunately, Allyne and one of the older boys, with their combined knowledge and application of mule psychology, were able to retrieve the freed and befuddled mule. She was led back to the hitching tree.

Besides teaching the regular program of the curriculum, Allyne presented plays and made all of the props and costumes. At Christmas time she presented a program that necessitated a snow scene. From some merchant in town she obtained a huge sheet of cardboard. In it she cut many small slots. We children shredded bundles of discarded newspapers. The cardboard was suspended at its four corners from the ceiling. The shredded paper was placed upon it. A string attached from the giant sifter afforded a hidden person to pull the string thereby producing a wonderful snow scene.

She also raised money for the school. Once she organized a "box supper". Each female from teenager to any unmarried woman prepared a delicious meal which usually consisted of sandwiches, fried chicken, a salad, a dessert or perhaps a pie or cake. The box was auctioned off to the highest bidder who shared the box with the maker of the box. I had never seen the young man who bought my box, but we ate together in stony silence.

The proceeds from the box supper went to expanding a library. The library consisted of thirty-three books having been bought by a previous teacher. I think that it was Miss Irene. Our library was enriched now by eight new boxes of books, each box containing twenty books. A globe was bought, too.

A rally was to be held. Today, it is called a field day. All of the county schools were invited to participate. Liberty School attended. We carried banners and yelled our cheers. "Stand them on their head! Stand them on their feet! Liberty School can't be beat!" I entered the recitation contest. Allyne made me a lavender and gold striped dress. I came in third. The girl from Gray who came in first in the 50 yard dash fainted as she crossed the finish line. Later that summer at a church meeting, a group of us got together and were introducing ourselves. The sprinter in the field day contest introduced herself thus, "My name is Ruby. I fainted at field day."

After completing the seventh grade, there was no more school to attend. There was no high school available when we finished the seventh grade. Allyne taught us again. She tried to teach us a little of the eight grade material. She introduced us to <u>Enoch</u>, <u>Arden</u>, <u>Snowbound</u> and <u>Evangeline</u>. By the end of the year, I was a year behind the girls my age. For no fault of hers, Sarah had fallen two years behind.

There were three elementary schools in the western part of Jones County. There were Liberty, Plentitude and Three Points and the patrons of these schools tried unsuccessfully to get the Board of Education to erect a high school in our section of the county. No funds. No school.

HIGH SCHOOL TRANSPORTATION

The next fall, Papa and Uncle Tom came up with a plan. By this time, Milton had purchased a Model-T Ford and had left it at home. Uncle Tom had purchased a car very much like it. It was decided that Sarah would drive our car with Mildred and me, go down to Uncle Tom's house, pick up Stanley and Frank and continue to Gray. The next week we would drive down, park our car at Uncle Tom's and ride with Stanley and Frank.

The itinerary took us back up to the Five Point Road, out to Wayside, Bradley and Gray. The roads were not paved. In fact, they were neither plated with grey dirt or with gravel. When it rained, the roads were muddy and slick. It was arranged that should there come a heavy rain that we could spend the night with a couple of residents there. I usually stayed with Sara Souther, who was a cousin of my cousin, Reba Jackson. The other place was with my friend, Ruby Gresham, who had moved to nearby Clinton.

The next year we rode a school bus.

We bus children were unable to participate in extracurricular activities. Yet those days were unforgettable. How the bus was obtained and how the driver was secured never crossed my mind. Blue Bird buses were not a common sight. Papa made the body for the first school bus that we rode. It was a box like contraption fifteen or twenty feet long. It was four or five feet high. A bench was built along each side and a double bench ran along the middle of it. For protection from the rain and the winter precipitation, a long roll of canvas was rolled up on each side and tied with a cord. In inclement weather, the canvas was rolled down and could be fastened securely. During our first few weeks of riding the bus, an unexpected shower arose. The driver stopped the bus and let the canvas roll down. Thinking that the shower would be over soon we climbed back into the bus and started toward home. The speed of the wind plus the speed of the bus caused the canvas to rise and fall. Someone likened it to the wings of an angel flopping. Someone suggested that we call the bus "Heaven Buggy" henceforth, it was called "Hea-fun Buggy".

A high school student drove the bus. Muddy roads were a major concern in those days. The bus driver always carried a shovel and axe. On one intensely cold morning the bus became mired in the mud. While the bus driver struggled to extricate us from the mud, we espied a fifty-pound lard can under the boughs of some bushes. We hurried out on half-frozen legs and brought it into the bus along with some dry leaves and dry sticks. Somebody had some matches. By the time the bus was out of the mud, we had a cozy fire warming us. I don't remember whether the smoke got into our eyes, or whether the fire just plainly burned out from the lack of fuel. It didn't matter for we had gotten warm.

The bus began its morning route at our mailbox at seven o'clock. We always left the house in ample time to get there. On inclement days, Papa insisted that we carry the wagon umbrella since we had no small umbrellas. When we had to share the huge umbrella, there was usually an embroilment. Mildred and I against Sarah whose legs were longer than ours and could walk faster.

One day, Mildred fell in the mud. The bus was chugging up the hill. Mildred wanted to go on to school, yet it was too far to go back to the house for a change. She boarded the bus. As we were en route to school, Mildred implored the bus driver to stop and wait on the roadside near her friend's home. The house was close to the road. She went in to Edna Barron (Graf)'s home, borrowed a dress, changed and proceeded to school.

One night after a deluge we started to school. (This was another year when we had a more mature driver.) We approached a creek, which ordinarily carried a flow of two or three inches of water, that had water four feet deep threatening the floor of the bridge. The bus driver went to the bridge, inspected it and its foundation. He returned to the bus affirming his belief that the bridge was substantial enough to bear the weight for the bus, but he wanted us all to get off the bus, let him drive across while we followed walking. We complied with his wishes, all but one of the older girls. She replied that she was not about to get off; that God has ordained her to die at some specified time; and that God would take her as she walked if He wanted to.

She and the bus driver rode across. Had I been a little smarter, I would have said, "Thou shalt not temp the Lord thy God."

Once again, the bus was mired in mud. While the driver was striving so hard to get out, we piled out and began playing in nearby pasture. It was beautiful out there.

Someone called to me. I began to walk toward her. There was a clump of briars between us. I felt that I could run right over the clump of briars. As I started, another voice called to me. I stopped to see what she wanted.

At that same instance, someone called out, "Here's an old well underneath this clump of briars." I shuddered to think how near I came to running into that old well. As I later related this to Aunt Matt, she said, "That was truly your Guardian Angel." I had never heard of Guarding Angel but as I thought back then and thought so many times since, I know that some Supernatural Power has saved me from impending disaster many times.

Often discussions were held on the bus. One day the discussion was around castor oil. One student said that he didn't mind taking castor oil. No one believed him. Later, he was challenged to crawl over the bus from one side to the other. He did. Each afternoon the bus stopped at a store in Clinton. Someone purchased a bottle of castor oil for his reward. It was handed over to RT who opened it, turned it up and swallowed it as if it were a soft drink. He was rewarded again with possibly a dollar in loose change contributed by his on-lookers.

The most likable boy on the bus was Don. As we approached his home one afternoon, we saw his father standing in the yard. As the bus stopped, the man waved his hat shouting cordial greetings. We all knew that he had been imbibing. I felt so sorry for Don. I would have been devastated with embarrassment had I been in Don's place. He merely said, "Pa's drunk again."

HIGH SCHOOL CLASSROOM AND CURRICULUM

The first day of school was a memorable one for us. There were thirty or more students in the eighth grade. The desks were single desks. I had not seen anything but double desks before. Nor had I ever seen such a disorderly class. All of the students were filled with talk and laughter.

The first period of the day was devoted to arithmetic which was taught by an elderly spinster called Miss May. I was a very poor student when it came to arithmetic. I must say that Miss May was the only teacher that I ever feared except Miss Irene. On the final test, I made a disgraceful 40 but I did pass.

One day, one of the boys was giggling about something. Perhaps it was sheer nervousness. Miss May ordered him to stop. He continued to giggle. Miss May picked up a book lying on the desk. With eyes flashing and glasses trembling on her nose, Miss May shouted, "If you don't shut up, I'll bust this English grammar book over your head!"

I expected to see momentarily the boy's brain scattered over the floor. On another occasion, the same boy brought a crow's foot to school. When the teacher stepped out of the room, he pulled the crow's foot out of his pocket and entertained the class by maneuvering the tendons in the crow's leg and making it dance.

Chapel exercises were held each morning with Mr. Bell, the presiding superintendent. He announced one morning that there were reports that there had been some smoking in the girls' outdoor privy and that it must be stopped. Miss May arose from her seat, and tears in her voice said, " I will hang my head in shame to think that there is a girl in Gray High School who would put a cigarette in her mouth."

Miss Akin, from Jenkinsburg, taught Algebra and Civics. Allyne had introduced me to Algebra so it was easy for me. When Miss Akin assigned us to bring in the names of the members of the Cabinet, that too, was easy. All that I did was to consult Willie who knew everything.

Mrs. Hattie E. Chiles taught English and Literature. I still feel that Miss Hattie and Allyne were the most efficient teachers that I ever had.

The thing that impressed me most when I entered high school was the amount of cheating that I saw was being done. During my eight years at Liberty School, I never saw cheating but once. Here, there were countless ways. One of the most common was copying another child's homework. Other ways were writing answers to the test questions on the soles of shoes, writing answers on slips of paper, writing answers on the dress slips, not to mention answers on hands and desks.

Only once did I cheat and that was not intentional. We were having a literature test. It was quite long. One question was to name the three types of poetry, describe each and give an example of each. I knew that I had a perfect paper with the exception of one word. I had known it before taking the test. As I sat there trying to remember that one word, the girl sitting in front of me turned around and I suspect that she wished to glean some information from my paper. She saw the blank space on my paper. She pursed her lips and formed the one word that I so desperately needed "Epic". Now I was really in a dilemma. Should I write the word or should I turn in the paper with a blank space? My Satanic nature won out. Years later when I was working on my Master's Degree and Miss Hattie was working on hers, she came to my apartment to have lunch with me. I confessed my cheating to her. She smiled. She neither condoned nor condemned my decision.

Mr. Bell was my Science teacher and a good one. The scientific principles that he taught gave me a firm foundation for learning other principles.

Mr. Knox succeeded Mr. Bell. He was young, probably fresh out of college. He taught geometry. The two years of algebra had been so easy for me. So was geometry. The only thing about my geometry course was that Mr. Knox gave numerical grades. When I handed in a paper without an error he would give me a grade of 99. Although I thought that I should receive 100%, Mr. Knox maintained that no one was perfect; therefore, no one could make 100.

For the senior year in high school, Mr. Perry Westbrooks was imported from Tennessee. He, too, was very young. All of the student body liked him. He knew and practiced his adolescent psychology. For the first time in Gray

High School's history, we had a football team. It was organized and coached by Mr. Westbrooks. We would all get excited when games were played and we were victorious. For the first time in my life, history came alive and was interesting.

There were times in which Mr. Westbrooks delivered sermonettes, and one which impressed me was: In high school, only the cream of the crop earns an "A". In college, it is only the cream of the cream of the crop that are given an "A".

This I found to be true. A few years later as a freshman, I saw many high school honor students weep and wail when she received a "B". It didn't dismay me for I remembered Mr. Westbrooks' lectures. I knew that I was not one of the most intelligent students. I knew that I had received my "A's" from hard work.

Another sermonette concerned spending money unnecessarily. "A rainy day would come, perhaps a trip to the dentist or a teacher demanding that a new book be purchased near the end of the term." I listened attentively and knew that I would have to watch my money carefully.

At the beginning of my senior year in high school, Uncle Dick Burden said, "If you graduate with first honors, I'll pay your way through college."

The honor came to me, not because I was brilliant, but because I burned the midnight oil and kept plugging along. Miss Hammock was a third grade teacher. She was assigned to me or I was assigned to her to write my valedictory address. I had not ever attended a graduation exercise, so I hadn't the slightest idea what to write about. She wrote it. I memorized it. Years later, I looked up the pronunciations of one word in the speech. To my chagrin, I had mispronounced the word "epitome".

COLLEGE

Preparation for college was an exciting experience. I chose Georgia State Teachers College, referred to usually as GSTC which was located in Athens, Georgia (Now University of Georgia). I knew that there were several other teaching training institutions which were equally good but several of my most admired friends were currently enrolled at GSTC.

During the summer I purchased a wardrobe trunk, the cost of which was $20.00. Allyne made me several pajamas and a pongee housecoat. Most people called them kimonos in those days. The uniforms consisted of twelve dresses for every day wear, a white dress for early fall and spring dress-up wear, a blue serge dress for Sunday dress-up wear, a dark navy blue coat, a fully pleated pair of black bloomers for gym, a white middy blouse, a pair of black tennis shoes, and matching stockings. The black bloomers were so fully pleated that they looked like a pleated skirt. This entire outfit was purchased from Michael's, a store located in Athens.

The everyday dresses were made of light tan material with darker tan collars and cuffs. There was a sewn-in pocket on each side of the dress with a pleat beneath it. The white dress was made exactly like it. The blue serge dress was perfectly plain. Freshman students from more affluent homes wore more beautiful and expensive clothes for the first several weeks. The excuse was that their uniforms had not come. The truth was that they had them already hanging in their closets. That did not bother me because I did not have any clothes that would impress anyone. I wore my uniform on enrollment day.

My only regret was that my pongee kimono was not nearly as attractive as those of the other girls. When I told Allyne at Christmas time about it, she told me to go to Burden, Smith and Company and get one, charging it to her account. I did. When I came home with my selection, Allyne was aghast at the price of it. It cost $10.00. It was a gorgeous black one with a brilliant Chinese design on it. Since it was Saturday night and I was leaving on Sunday, there was no way to exchange it. The remainder of my stay at college as I wore it, I suffered two feelings: one was that I was as well-dressed as anyone in college as far as clothes were concerned; and the other was a remorse for having plunged Allyne so deeply into debt.

There were five dormitories on campus. I applied for and was assigned to Gilmer Hall where my Jones County friends were situated. I was place on the same floor and I was in a room adjoining them. The matron-in-charge was Miss Nellie, a lady with a Victorian mien.

The daily plan for the day was something like this. A wake-up bell rang at seven o'clock. We had until seven-thirty to dress and get our room in order. At that time we walked to the dining hall. There, ten girls were assigned to each table. That was the table which we must occupy for the next six weeks, three times a day. A Senior sat at the end of each table. A blessing was sung by the entire student body. After the blessing was sung, we sat down to eat. A pre-appointed senior checked each table for absentees. Woe to anyone who had not appeared. We had thirty minutes to eat, return to our room, get our books and get to our eight o'clock class. While not in class, we were on our own, to go to the library or to our room.

In the evening, extracurricular meetings were held. Bible classes were held. There was a club for almost every subject. During the afternoon and until nine o'clock one could sign up for a bath. A sign-up sheet was posted at the door of the bathroom. We were allowed fifteen minutes for a bath. From the time of the evening meal until nine-thirty, one was expected to be either at a club meeting or in the room studying.

The rules stated that one could not go off campus at any time unchaperoned. On Monday afternoon, Miss Nellie chaperoned her girls to go across the street where a little grocery store and a drug store were located.

There was so little to buy and so little money with which to buy. Usually I bought one pound of peanut butter in bulk for ten cents. My roommates bought saltines or some other commodities to supplement the snack. On alternate Mondays, we were allowed to go up town in groups of two or three. Of course, we were well chaperoned with a matron. We were restricted to shopping in two blocks up town. Although I had no money to spend, I went for the change of scenery of the campus.

On Sundays, Sunday school and church were in order. One could walk to Sunday school but if one wished to attend church only, she would have to ride the bus. We all met on the corner of the campus on Sunday morning. We formed a line long enough to look like a modern line of protestors, about six hundred of us. We lined up in accordance to the church we were attending and its proximity. I usually attended the First Baptist Church but some days when a test was looming nearby, I would slip a few French or Spanish verbs into my handbag and stop at the church nearest the campus. A sermon of Hell and damnation was preached at that particular church and I could get into a back corner, close my ears and study my verbs.

On Sunday afternoons, we were allowed to go out on the front campus and watch the traffic go by. Or we could go to our rooms and write letters or read or date.

If a girl was brave enough to have a boyfriend over, she would be allowed two hours with him within the confines of the parlor where the matron darted in every so often to see that everything was going as her Victorian training had prescribed.

One Jones County girl was surprised to learn that her boyfriend was in town. I don't know how they arranged for a date on Sunday afternoon. Using the usual procedure she needed a written permit from her mother. She had her roommate to write the permit and hurried to the dean's office to have it okayed. She thought that she had lied convincingly when she assured the dean that it had arrived in the morning's mail. The final question that he asked her was how had her mother contrived to mail the permit without folding the paper. Permit denied!

A spring day arrived on which a state athletic meet was being held on the University campus. A teacher from Gray came by to see my roommate, Sara. She offered to take Sara and me to the meet. Sara introduced her to Miss Nellie who readily allowed us to go with her to enjoy the competition.

When the activities were over, the teacher announced that she must hurry back to Gray. Could we possibly ride the bus back to the dorm? Fortunately, we both had the financial resources but what would the authorities say if they saw two sophomores riding home unchaperoned? This could be an expulsion offense. Fortunately, everything went well. We did not alight from the bus directly in front of our dorm, but went to the next stop which was barely on the campus. We practically ran to the dorm, changed clothes, and trotted down to the dining room just a second before the door closed.

On Friday nights, we were served fried fish followed by ice cream. A relative of mine had always warned me never to eat fish and ice cream at the same meal. For three years, 700 girls ate fish and ice cream every Friday night and no one ever became sick. Saturday night was hot dog night. Many of us could and would eat five hot dogs for supper and some would sneak out another five for a late night snack.

Chapel attendance was compulsory. Here again we were assigned seats and were checked to verify our presence. The two public school music teachers alternately led the singing. Each of us were required to have a chapel song book. The songs that I remember most vividly were Faith of our Fathers, Drink to Me Only, With Thine Eyes, and Believe Me Thou Endearing Young Charms. There was one ever present elderly teacher who sat in the back of the auditorium and rattled her keys.

Although we did not have to observe study hall on Saturday nights, we students from Jones County and some from Jasper County became so filled with ennui, we planned some excitement. We planned that one girl could climb out the window, go to the mini- porch, deposit a bottle which had held some wine for menstrual cramps, and rattle the door. The bottle was laid on the doorstep to add evidence to the prank. All of the girls would yell and run into the hall while the bottle-placer, door rattler scampered back into her room. We all knew that Miss Nellie went for a bath at a scheduled time. We would wait until she was comfortably enjoying her ablution. All went as planned. Miss Allen, the assistant matron came scurrying down from the third floor. She was a petite red-head, endowed with a fiery temper. Miss Allen wanted to know what the noise was. Each girl tried to talk at once telling what she had heard. I appeared to be frightened and produced a copious amount of tears. Sara Allen who was a more mature and respected student said, "It's a little Beatrice Jarrell. She's such a nervous child."

Miss Allen came over to console me saying, "It was just a rascally University of Georgia boy trying to frighten you girls."

Miss Allen had blown her little referee whistle to summon the night watchman. He came. He found the bottle and confirmed Miss Allen's suspicions.

You would be surprised at the number of girls living in Bradwell Hall who declared that she had seen a young man run from Gilmore Hall.

In preparing to go to Sunday school the next morning, one of the girls participating in the hoax became conscience-stricken and announced that she was going to the matron and confess the hoax. It took the threatening and coaxing of the other sixteen girls to convince her that everyone of us would be shipped. The word "shipped" connoted that we all would be expelled. I think it was our threat of what we would do to her that prevented confession.

The Freshmen and Sophomores were all required to take gym. We carried our bloomers and gym shoes around to class until gym time. We were allotted a few minutes in which to change clothing. Everything had to be apple-pie order in the dressing room. The gym teacher inspected it fairly regularly. She was stricter than Miss May who I had endured in the eighth grade but was not nearly as old.

In addition to marching, we were drilled on many folk dances. If I had had any sense of rhythm, it could have been a most enjoyable period. One day, the teacher asked me on which foot a certain dance started. I replied, "I don't know" which was the truth. She then called on another student who replied, "Left."

In a most sarcastic voice, the teacher said, "I had rather had someone say left and get it wrong like Miss Creter did than to say I don't know."

Twice weekly, a session called Athletics was held. It was strictly voluntary. An older teacher directed this activity. She was firm but made things be pleasant and we had fun.

When Field Day was announced on a beautiful spring day, we found that the P.E. teachers had it well-planned. Only those involved in athletics participated. The competition was between classes. The events scheduled were the fifty and hundred yard dash, relays, a basketball game, a captain ball game, and a volleyball game. Each year I was a member of the volleyball team and several of the relays.

There were good teachers and there were poor teachers at Teachers College. I did not feel that the best that I had, surpassed either Allyne or Miss Hattie Childs in Gray.

One of the courses in which I learned most was Public School Music. I had been reared in a home where there was no music except what we gleaned from the Edison phonograph. I had absolutely no musical talent or ability. I had no idea what a high note or a low note meant. We were given a comprehensive test to reveal our musical knowledge and musical ability. I am sure that no one had ever made a score as low as I made on that test. As I studied the book on music theorem, I began to learn something about music. A piano was available. With the help of the piano and illustrations in the book, I did learn something. By the end of the term I had learned to transpose America into any of the major scales. In later years, I learned to play simple exercises on the violin.

During my sophomore year, I was required to take a course called Fundamentals of Speech. I had been told that Miss Vance, the teacher, was a terror. That was among my college days greatest surprises. It was one of my most enjoyable courses. I acquired an "A" in the course.

Just when the Great Depression began, I cannot quite remember. Being in college with my expenses paid, I did not feel the brunt of the depression as others in my family or as some of my college friends.

One winter, after boarding the train at Round Oak to return to school, I saw a friend of mine weeping torrents of tears. She had either borrowed money or was on a scholarship to finance her education. Her widowed mother and younger sister were at home almost destitute. Her sister was too young to secure a job. Her widowed mother was an accomplished dressmaker but in a small town there were few people who could afford the services of a dressmaker. My friend's brother had graduated from high school and was working one or two days each week at the A & P Grocery. He was the sole support of the three.

My family had food to eat but no money for such commodities as sugar, salt, lard and other things not provided by the garden. Taxes were to be paid. Milton was cut back to only one or two days per week at his job for the railroad. In some miraculous way, Milton paid the taxes, thereby saving the farm.

Charlie was completely laid off from his job on the railroad. He finally located a job firing a boiler at a plant to dye yarn in East Juliette.

One inadequate teacher that I had was a French teacher. I really do not understand how she had secured a French teaching status. She was past middle-age, wore thick glasses and sat sedately at her desk. She opened her book. We did the same. She read, "L'homme marche."

We repeated, "L'homme marche."
She read, "Le cheval trotte."
We repeated, "Le cheval trotte."

And so on for the entire period. She gazed at her book and spoke in a nasal whiney voice. Each day several students slipped out of the room unobserved. Very little French did I learn from that woman. The next year, French Teacher #1 did not return. I'll bet I can guess why. French Teacher #2 babbled non-stop in fluent French. When she walked up to me and said, "Bon jour mademoiselle, comment allez vous…?" I knew exactly what she meant but could not think of the first French word. I replied politely in my very best Spanish, "Muy bein, gracias y usted?" She then knew that I was hopeless as far as French was concerned. I worked so hard on French but I made very little progress. In spite of it all I think that she liked me. She told that she was going to give me a "D" (a low passing grade) on the promise that I would never tell anyone that she had taught me French.

Biology was another of my favorite subjects. I had been advised to stay clear of it…advice from a friend. The instructor was past middle age. He had unique methods of teaching. For instance, he graded on questions that we asked in class. Of course, we studied hard to enable us to ask sensible questions. He stated that we could get bored and cut class. That would be OK with him, but we must not cut on account of illness. Illness was inexcusable! If we followed the health rules such as eating properly, sleeping adequately, and exercising daily, we would not get sick. If one felt a cold coming on, get out, work up a sweat, take a hot bath and rest in bed an hour. I tried it and it worked.

"Everything is poisonous, yet nothing is poisonous", he would often quote. What triggered that off was that the newspaper and also the radio told of a woman who was turning an orange color. The doctors were baffled. When on her death bed it was learned that she had eaten a bunch of carrots for six months or longer. "In like manner", he told us, "if one would place a teaspoon of cobra venom in a barrel of water, stir it, take a teaspoon from that barrel and stir it in a second barrel of water...take a spoonful of that and inject it into a human, it will not hurt the human." I wondered if he had tried it, but that was a question I dared not ask.

At the end of my sophomore year, most of my Jones County friends had completed their education or were moving to other dormitories. I transferred to Senior Hall. The matron there was sweet and understanding. She did not act like a warden in the Federal Penitentiary.

Mildred joined me that year. We roomed together and had one other roommate. It was so much more pleasant here in Senior Hall.

Early one morning, we heard the telephone ring. Both Mildred and Iris said jokingly, "It's for me." I had the most eerie feeling that it was for me. Sure enough my name was called. It was Annie Florence telling me that Ida Belle had passed away. Annie was living some thirty miles north of Athens. She came shortly and we all went home for the funeral.

Later in the year, Annie Florence invited us out to spend a weekend with her. Norah was a toddler. Some child's program was presented at the school. We attended. The air was filled with coughing and whooping. Whooping cough! Mildred had had it but I had not. Annie thought that we both had had it. At any rate, I developed it. I told no one except Mildred and our roommate. I could not stand the thought of having to be quarantined and lose and entire quarter from school. When I had a paroxysm of coughing, I would leave the classroom or the table until it resided. It lasted approximately six weeks. I believe that was the longest six weeks of my life.

Everyone was required to take the course **The Constitution of the United States**. Our teacher, Miss Spit Fire, was reputed to be the most brilliant teacher in the state of Georgia, or perhaps the United States. She was said to have been so precocious that she had been accepted in a most elite and prestigious boys' school in England. She was passed middle-aged. She had bright red hair and snapping green eyes. She was barely five feet tall and three feet wide. She had a platform approximately ten feet square. She often wore a pongee dress which drooped in front. It drooped so much that Mildred feared that she would get her foot entangled and tumble off her throne. Usually a wisp of hair fell into her face. She scribbled on the blackboard underlining half of the words she wrote. When one could not decipher a word, she declared emphatically that it was as clear as print.

Miss Spit Fire had a vocabulary that a veteran sailor could be proud of. I heard her say one day, "Why don't you stick your head out that window and air your damned brains?" One girl had a vestige of hair growing on her upper lip. Miss Spit Fire called her "Miss Pussy Cat Whiskers".

Nearly every afternoon, she called someone to come to her office at 5:30. My day came. This is the gist of her speech to me, "Miss Jarrell, you are not doing well in this class. I don't know whether you study enough or whether you are interested in it. But I think that you don't have sense enough to learn it. Go think it over and let me know." I never returned. When my friend was called in, she also received a barrage of "I don't know why" but ended up saying, "I don't think YOU PRAY ENOUGH. Get down on your knees and pray." Opal complied with the order. She too passed.

Mildred was standing around the blackboard when she had her "interview" with Miss Spit Fire. She was lambasted because she didn't have an outline in her notebook. It ended with Miss Spit Fire throwing the notebook at her and saying, "Here take your faulty old notebook."

One day, Miss Spit Fire began to sneeze. I lost count by the time I reached ten. Everyone was restraining themselves to keep from laughing. I scrunched down behind the girl in front of me. It did little good. Edna was as thin as a little reed and was quivering like a little reed in swift water. By the time that Miss Spit Fire's sneezes reached around twenty, everybody was twittering. Miss Spit Fire began to cry and said, "Here I am about to take pneumonia and you all are laughing at me."

On the University campus, she taught a class composed largely of boys. It was told that as school was dismissed at Christmas holidays, she stood at the door and handed each boy a card which had been sent to her the previous Christmas.

One Sunday, I decided to visit the First Methodist Church. I was shuttled off into Miss Spit Fire's Sunday school class. I was amazed! She preached a wonderful sermon on race relations! She did as well as Billy Sunday or Gypsy Smith, the leading evangelists of that era.

It was during my junior year at Teachers College that I was inducted into the Quadrangle, an honorary scholastic society. It had been hard work, not superior mental ability that had caused it.

The end of my junior year at Teachers College was marked by a metamorphosis as significant as the Industrial Revolution was to Europe.

The Board of Regents saw fit to integrate Georgia State Teachers College with the University of Georgia. Gone were the uniforms. Gone were the rigid rules. Happy were the students!

For my senior year, I was sent to the University of Georgia campus. I was assigned to live in Milledge Hall, one of the newer dorms at that time. It was located only a few hundred yards from the entrance to Sanford Stadium. My roommate was a talker and a daughter of a Baptist minister. Here there were only two students for each room. There was no limit to when we could take showers. There must have been rules and regulations. The only one that I remember was to be in the dorm by eleven o'clock. So that didn't faze me at all.

Students often had classes on the former GSTC campus with only five or ten minutes between classes. How did we get to classes in such a short period of time? We stood at a designated corner and thumbed rides. All of the townspeople knew of the problem and they practiced being instigated and very kindly cooperated.

For winter quarter of my senior year, I began Shakespeare and Student Teaching. I was assigned to teach sixth grade English. The critic teacher was strict and not so friendly. I taught one day feeling half sick. She bawled me out about some little trivial matter. The next day I was unable to teach. For the following four weeks, I was terrible sick. I wondered if I had taken measles as a child, would I have been that sick.

In this epidemic, it seemed that every victim had ear trouble. In fact, two students died from the complications of the ears and brain. I know that I was delirious part of the time because I thought I was two people. Mama could not come up and care for me. The infirmary nurse did all that she could to make me comfortable. There was another co-ed in the room with me. Her mother came up to wait on her and also helped me some. When I was dismissed from the infirmary, I wondered how I could make up four or five weeks of work.

Before I had gone to the infirmary, we had studied only one Shakespearean play. I met a student who contrived to get a copy of the one and only test that had been given. We studied the test. I made a "B" on the course. How lucky could I get!

The critic teacher had a contrite heart for having scolded me severely when I was taking the measles. She let me make up the work by assigning me to correct and grade thirty-five workbooks. For doing this, she gave me a grade of "B" for Practice Teaching when I had taught only one day.

For my Spring Quarter, I needed to take only two subjects. One was Introduction to Psychology at eight o'clock and an education course at nine o'clock. By ten o'clock I was free for the day. The class in psychology was interesting but would have been more so had not the instructor been so old. He talked with his mouth almost closed and his lips not moving. I sat on the front row and strained my almost deaf ears to hear him. I studied the two books and earned another "B".

The last course was an education course from an instructor whom I had for several previous courses. He graded on the curve always. He usually gave two "A's" from three to fifteen "B's" and the rest "C's". I don't think that he ever gave a failing grade. I didn't bother to study. Before the test, I read the titles of each chapter and the sub-titles. On the day of the test, I was among the median to finish. As I gathered my belongings to go, I kept watching him from the corner of my eye. He picked up my completed paper, looked at the name, opened his grade book and wrote a "B" in it. Sure enough, that was the grade I received on my report card. Other students used the same tactics to foretell their grades.

When I returned to my room at ten o'clock, I was really "babied". I was required to go next door to the dining room and drink a huge glass of milk with cream an inch thick. Next, I was instructed to go to my room for bed rest until one o'clock when lunch was served.

I graduated from the University of Georgia in 1934.

After Papa's death in January 1958 and Mama's death in February 1958, the United States Government wished to buy the land that lay east of the River Road. They did not wish to give the amount that we thought we should get. When we learned that the government was going to condemn the land and give us a low price, we sold it to Georgia Pacific Lumber Company.

We all agreed that we did not want to split up the belongings of what was left of the farm, so we decided to dedicate it to the State of Georgia so generations to come could get a glimpse at life as it was on the Jarrell farm in rural Georgia many years ago.

Beatrice Jarrell Bittaker
April 02, 1912 - November 19, 1997

Beatrice graduated from the University of Georgia (UGA) in 1934. Later she returned to receive a specialist degree at UGA after obtaining her master's degree from Mercer University.

TID BITS

It seems that we had far more rain in those days than we have today. Mama called these several days of rain a freshet. During one of these freshets, the rain covered the bridges to the extent that the mail could not be delivered. Someone on the west side of Falling Creek went to the flooded bridge, waded across, picked up the mail for the patrons on the west side and delivered it. At one time the road became so muddy that the axle of the buggy drug the ground.

****

When we were small, a favorite between meal snack was boley-holey biscuits. To fashion one of these biscuits one of the biscuits was held on its side. With the index finger, a hole was bored in to the biscuit. Syrup was poured in until the hole was filled. Naturally, the syrup was poured slowly so that as much syrup as possible would be absorbed.

****

When Papa learned that it would be mandatory that everyone would be required to have birth certificates, he went to Gray and obtained the blanks necessary for him to fill out an application for every child. I had learned to type. Papa asked me to fill them and he signed them. Since I had only two names, Beatrice Jarrell, I typed my name as Martha Beatrice Jarrell.

****

A case of smallpox was discovered near Gray. Mama somehow scraped up a quarter each for us to be vaccinated. As the days progressed so did our vaccinated spot. It became very sore. I accidentally scraped mine causing the crust to come off. Mama scraped up another ten cents for me to have a shield that protected the lesion from coming into contact with other jostling friends and protecting it from the sweater's harsh sleeve.

****

It was only about five miles from our house to that of Aunt Florrie, Mama's sister. By traveling by buggy it required over an hour to reach her house. So you see, Mama visited her sister only once or twice a year. How I did enjoy that visit! It may be that it was because I was so hungry by the time that dinner was served. You will notice that I said "dinner"; that is, in those days there were three meals: breakfast, dinner and supper.

****

There are a lot of known facts about the Jarrell Plantation that few today know about. At one time, when I was a child, there were so few trees between us and Aunt Matt's house, that we could see the train as it made its nocturnal trip northward.

****

There was a cemetery near the Holland home. I could never understand why Sarah and Charlie became interested in reading the epitaph on the tombstone, but they did. Each afternoon they vied for who could say it accurately first. Sarah can still repeat it this day. I am sure that Charlie retained that un-vital information to his dying day.

****

Just east of the woodpile and adjacent to the pasture fence, Papa once built a pigpen in which he kept the hogs until slaughtering time. Later, the next summer Mildred and I constructed an air-conditioned playhouse by placing boards across the top of it.

****

Papa had a watermelon hole dug about thirty feet south of the playhouse. In the very early morning, cool watermelons were hauled in and placed in this cool storage place. In the mid-afternoon we enjoyed the delicious watermelons atop our playhouse.

****

When Sarah was driving Pet, we were told the aging but faithful old horse must never rush. One day Sarah clicked the reins and urged Pet to trot. Two days later we suffered a tongue-lashing from Papa. Aunt Julie told Papa that Sarah was urging the poor old horse to gallop. Sarah denied the charges but Papa maintained that Julie did not lie.

****

Once we had a bull whose name was Toby. He was so ferocious that when we heard him outside the pasture, we fled in terror. Once when Mildred and I heard him, we climbed the nearest tree. We waited for him to pass by. He never came. What we had heard was the bellowing of a bullfrog.

****

Once Willie inadvertently fastened Papa up in the back mule stall. He did not learn about it until several hours later when the irate parent came in. We didn't know how he could have possible escaped. I didn't dare ask him until several years later. When I asked him, he did not remember.

****

At sometime during my early years at school, the daily paper predicted the coming of a total eclipse of the sun. It happened during the afternoon. As darkness fell upon the face of the earth, the cows came home lowing and the chickens hastened to the chicken house to their roosting poles. It seemed to me that it was dark a long time. Eventually, daylight appeared. Things resumed to normal.

****

Aunt Florrie's youngest child was Frank who was only six months younger than I. He was such a friendly little host in entertaining us with his little red wagon. Frank had a little kitten named "Hard Times". He had found it greatly abused and had nursed it back to health.

****

Pet, our faithful horse, and who had ferried all eleven children to and from school was turned out to pasture. The term, "turned out to pasture" connotated that he was retired. He would no longer be required or be expected to work. He would spend the rest of his days in the pasture thinking about the good old days.

****

We had intelligent cats. Whenever they heard knives being sharpened, they made haste to the sound. They knew that Mama was about to slaughter chickens and goodies would be given to them.

****

One summer, Aunt Annie gave me a pair of ducks. I thought the little ducklings were so cute. Previously, I could not understand why Mama had always frowned upon having ducks, geese, guineas and turkeys. I soon found out why ducks were not welcomed fowls. Since there were no nearby ponds or streams, the ducks kept the chickens' drinking water unfit for chicken consumption. After a year or two of tolerating them, we ate them.

****

At one time, the boys built and painted a boat with creosote to deter erosion. Not only did it deter erosion but surprisingly it induced blistering of the skin of those who swam around it. We all had blistered faces, necks and arms.

****

Some months after Mary visited us, she and Richard were married. We welcomed the lovely and witty girl into our family. A year later, Mama and Papa's first grandchild was born. How we all rejoiced! James was the sweetest baby and the most beloved child that ever existed, we thought. We all doted on James who was a precocious child. When he was a year old, he could say over a hundred twenty words.

CPSIA information can be obtained
at www.ICGtesting.com
Printed in the USA
LVHW051028040720
659731LV00004B/466